from here to e

READY TO

.COMPETE?

from here to e

equip yourself for a career in the wired
economy

Lisa Khoo

www.yourmomentum.com

the stuff that drives you

What is momentum?

Momentum is a completely new publishing philosophy, in print and online, dedicated to giving you more of the information, inspiration and drive to enhance who you are, what you do, and how you do it.

Fusing the changing forces of work, life and technology, momentum will give you the bright stuff for a brighter future and set you on the way to being all you can be.

Who needs momentum?

Momentum is for people who want to make things happen in their career and their life, who want to work at something they enjoy and that's worthy of their talent and their time. Momentum people have values and principles, and question who they are, what they do, and who for. Wherever they work, they want to feel proud of what they do. And they are hungry for information, stimulation, ideas and answers ...

Momentum online

Visit *www.yourmomentum.com* to be part of the talent community. Here you'll find a full listing of current and future books, an archive of articles by momentum authors, sample chapters and self-assessment tools. While you're there, post your worklife questions to our momentum coaches and sign up to receive free newsletters with even more stuff to drive you.

More momentum

If you need more drive for your life, try one of these titles, all published under the momentum label:

change activist
make big things happen fast
Carmel McConnell

lead yourself
be where others will follow
Mick Cope

happy mondays
putting the pleasure back into work
Richard Reeves

the big difference
life works when you choose it
Nicola Phillips

hey you!
pitch to win in an ideas economy
Will Murray

snap, crackle or stop
change your career and create your own
destiny
Barbara Quinn

float you
how to capitalize on your talent
Carmel McConnell & Mick Cope

coach yourself
make real change in your life
Tony Grant & Jane Greene

innervation
redesign yourself for a smarter future
Guy Browning

grow your personal capital
what you know, who you know and how you
use it
Hilarie Owen

PEARSON EDUCATION LIMITED

Head Office
Edinburgh Gate
Harlow CM20 2JE
Tel: +44 (0)1279 623623
Fax: +44 (0)1279 431059

London Office:
128 Long Acre, London WC2E 9AN
Tel: +44 (0)20 7447 2000
Fax: +44 (0)20 7240 5771
Website: www.business-minds.com

First published in Great Britain in 2001

© Pearson Education Limited 2001

ISBN 1843 04008 5

British Library Cataloguing in Publication Data
A CIP catalogue record for this book can be obtained from the British Library.

10 9 8 7 6 5 4 3 2 1

Typeset by Northern Phototypesetting Co. Ltd, Bolton
Printed and bound in Great Britain by Biddles Ltd, Guildford and King's Lynn

Cover design by Heat
Text design by Heat and Claire Brodmann Book Designs, Lichfield, Staffs

The Publishers' policy is to use paper manufactured from sustainable forests.

opening

introduction / xix

part one
the new world

part two
the skills you need

part three
opportunities

chapter 9
jobs in depth: web jobs / 66

part four
acquiring new skills

chapter 13
e-commerce explained / 94

part five
moving forward

part six
in their own words:
new economy players speak

chapter 19

what new economy workers have to say / 154

closing

introduction

page xviii / xix

'I work in whatever medium likes me at the moment.'

Marc Chagall, painter

So we've all heard there's an economic revolution underway, that the internet, e-commerce and dot coms are changing what we do and how we do it, that it's the most fundamental transformation since the industrial age. We've heard there are new jobs out there and that they're cutting-edge, creative, and lucrative – and the people at the forefront doing them, pushing the boundaries, setting the new standards, are modern-day pioneers.

This isn't just a book about getting a job in a dot.com. It's about getting a job for the future in an increasingly wired world. Soon all businesses will be e-businesses. And that will be very soon indeed – if a business doesn't have an effective website right now, it's already at a significant disadvantage in reaching and serving customers. Much has been made of the 'dotbombs' as they have come to be known, but the dotcoms with a sound business model and sound management have survived and there will be many more. Don't let it put you off getting yourself e-literate. It's a competitive advantage.

We have used the term 'new economy' throughout the book. Already some people are saying that the new economy has been succeeded by what has been variously dubbed: the 'next economy', the 'new new economy', the 'wired economy', the 'knowledge economy' and so on.

What you call it doesn't really matter. That e-skills will be a major part of the success of people within it do matter. And that's what this book's about.

And you're wondering – is there a place in that brand new world for you? If you want to play the game, be part of the action, what are the new rules?

Over the course of the past decade, technological change has created a new system of values, placing a premium on work associated with information and knowledge ahead of manual labour and the assembly line. In some ways, work has never looked so good. It's not just the jobs that have changed, so has our attitude towards them. Corporate careers are being replaced by portfolio careers and being your own boss. The New Economy needs new ideas, and new ways of thinking are critical. New business models are needed, along with the new businesspeople to run them.

'The internet – and what it will become in the next two or three decades – is something that we have yet to fully grasp and understand. At the moment it is like the "Wild West" – anarchic, exciting, full of amazing opportunities. There is no doubt we are at the beginning of a 30-year revolution on the scale of the Industrial Revolution.'

Marcus Marcou, Managing Director, BusinessesForSale.com

Ask yourself:

◆ Do you feel understimulated at work?

◆ Are you ambitious but not moving up the corporate ladder fast enough?

◆ Are you curious about how technology can transform the future?

◆ Are you a self-motivated hard worker, unafraid of long hours?

- Do you embrace change, not fear it?

- Are you longing for a chance to show what you can really do?

If yes is your answer on all counts, the New Economy is the place for you. It's exciting, challenging and, best of all, the jobs are available, not just in areas like computer programming but all along the dot com hierarchy. You may be surprised at how qualified you already are, and how easy it is to skill up in areas that you're missing. By setting yourself goals to build on your basic talents you can join the wave of the future.

'It's the end of the world as we know it and I feel fine.'

REM, from the Album *Document*

What this book will do is introduce you to the new world of work – its pros and its cons – and show you what kinds of jobs are out there, what skills are in demand, and how you can get them. With this book as your virtual career counsellor, you'll be able to set yourself on course to the e-career of your dreams.

In the first three chapters we will give you the **bird's-eye view** of the state of the New Economy, its **job market** and its basic requirements; we will also introduce you to some people who have already made the transition to the dot com or e-commerce world, and they'll tell you **in their own words** what they look for in **prospective employees**. We'll follow that with an **assessment** of what skills you have and what ones you don't and we'll point you to further chapters so you can fill in the blanks, covering areas such as **e-commerce** and **lifelong learning**, as well as how to learn basic **computer** and **technology skills**. We will cut through the jargon and take a look at what the **jobs actually are** in core **IT** and peripheral areas such as **marketing** and **sales**, based on real adverts. We'll look at some **salary scales** and other core **benefits** you can expect. Once you're ready to make the move, we'll go over where to start, where to **look for jobs** that are publicized and how to find them when they're not. You'll hear from people who have already made **successful transitions**. Leading **recruitment agencies** will share with you their hot **job trends** and advice.

Be warned, it is a roller coaster out there. Like any industry in a state of flux, the future is still being formed, it's evolving. Wherever possible this book will point you to the way ahead, tell you what current conventional wisdom is, what the latest projections are from the players and the pundits, explode the hype and dismantle the myths. But it's changing at the speed of light. Even as you read this, it has turned another corner. We think that makes it exciting – fascinating even. If a bit of that's for you, read on.

01

part one
the new world

'It is not the strongest of the species that survive, nor the most intelligent, but the ones most responsive to change.'

Charles Darwin

chapter one
so what's it all about then?

the new work world

◆ Characteristics

◆ Who's got it?

◆ Just how big is it?

◆ The UK situation

◆ Observations on the New Economy

NEW ECONOMY SNAPSHOT

By 2004 there are expected to be 200–250 million European internet users and 22 million households online, according to Jupiter Research.

The New Economy has already had a profound impact not just on the jobs we do, but on how we do them. For the better part of this century the majority of jobs were in the manufacturing industry handling mass production in hierarchical organizations. Now, according to a US government report, 80 per cent of people in the

USA – 93 million people – do not spend their days making things: they work in jobs requiring them to move things, process or generate information or provide services to people.

Characteristics

The New Economy is high-tech, service-oriented and office-based. It's also:

◆ **Idea-based:** The need for companies to constantly innovate has created a seemingly insatiable appetite for the people who can think out-of-the-box. Ideas are the currency of the New Economy.

◆ **Knowledge-oriented:** This has driven the need for education and training high up on the list of priorities, both in general and highly specialized areas, as automation replaces many traditional labour-intensive jobs.

◆ **Technology-driven:** The latest scientific innovations now determine whether a company can survive and prosper.

◆ **Dynamic and adaptable:** Old Economy companies were stable and static, following well-established best practices. Today's economy is fluid and constantly evolving. Having a corporate culture that can adapt and be flexible is fundamental.

◆ **Constantly innovating:** With value no longer exclusively determined by the supply and demand of labour and capital, ideas and people provide the competitive advantage. A company's rate of creative destruction – its ability to drop unsuccessful models and embrace something new – is directly related to its success.

◆ **Speedy:** Conventional wisdom says time on the web is about one fourth of real time. In other words, your business should do in one quarter what traditional companies do in one year. This has profound implications for the way businesses operate, down to how your basic structure should work.

◆ **Entrepreneurial:** America has long been seen as the bastion of entrepreneurial culture, but Europe is beginning to shed its traditionally risk-averse attitude. The New Economy functions on a trial and error basis. Successful companies are putting aside a fear of failure and realizing that it's more important to fail and gain experience along the way, than to never try at all, which guarantees failure.

NEW ECONOMY SNAPSHOT

The New Economy is having an impact on large companies but it's the small and medium-sized ones that have found the new rules most advantageous. PricewaterhouseCoopers' 2000 European Benchmarking Study for technology companies says, 'Traditionally it was the large global players that formerly had an advantage over small companies in terms of economies of scale and access to resources. Now the internet is diminishing these advantages by making it possible for any company to do business globally. At the same time smaller companies have the advantage of not being burdened with expensive infrastructure, heavy bureaucracy, resistance to change and a suffocating hierarchy.'

◆ **Multiskilled:** Since the workplace is less hierarchical in the New Economy, employees who have a range of skills are critical. Small dot coms in particular need people who can swarm from one troublespot to another. Everyone has to be prepared to get his or her hands dirty. Staff need to have both the capability and inclination to adopt a lifelong learning plan.

◆ **All about attitude:** The pioneering instinct is strong among those most successful in the New Economy so far, perhaps because a sense of satisfaction drives people to perform better, perhaps because passion makes vision possible. Determination, enthusiasm, passion, creativity have eclipsed experience as the favourite skill set.

◆ **Global:** On the web, national boundaries are irrelevant. Your customers don't care what country you are in, only that you can deliver to theirs. Be prepared to play in many markets, not just pan-European ones. In the Old Economy, companies needed only to be successful on a national stage – now, it is essential to be integrated into the world economy.

People who already do business in Europe enjoy a natural advantage in the region's internet economy, which is simultaneously local, regional and global. 'No one else can understand this like Europeans,' International Data Corporation's Senior Vice President John Gantz said. Gantz says because European companies have a history of dealing with and understanding the cultural difference, they're well equipped to cope with it online. 'Europe's prospects have not looked so good in decades,' he said.

◆ **Networked:** (As in computer network, where all users are in contact with each other.) Within companies, all parts are in communication with one another, no longer separated by reporting structures. Project management is performed in teams. With the decline of the monolithic company comes the rise of the partnership, the association, and the strategic alliance. Outsourcing is routine. Personal networks are even more important.

◆ **Digital:** The driving technology is not the factory floor, it's the ability to transform information into bits and bytes. This is the cornerstone of the New Economy, the final implications of which we haven't yet begun to understand.

Who's got it?

While America is in the lead in developing a New Economy, predictions are that its growth will level off, allowing the rest of the world to catch up. By 2005, 245 million households worldwide will be online and the biggest growth areas will be outside of the USA, according to a Jupiter Media Metrix report.

Increasingly the internet is being seen as a vital business tool, not just by dot coms whose existence is wholly dependent on the internet, but by traditional companies looking to add the internet to the list of ways they distribute and market their goods.

the new world

from here to e

momentum

'With the revolution in IT the European economy is being transformed from standardized manual production to a more diversified, knowledge-based production of goods and services. If this trend is followed to its logical conclusion, millions of jobs will be created in IT while millions of other less skilled positions will be lost.'

Datamonitor research group

Some American dot coms are casting their eyes to the European market, and the region appears poised to become one of the most dynamic in the future.

Market research group eMarketer predicts that by 2003 the number of Western European internet users will grow to nearly 105 million, accounting for 34 per cent of the adult population.

NEW ECONOMY SNAPSHOT

IDC predicts that by 2004 the economic value of e-commerce in Europe should be 89 per cent that of the United States, compared with 13 per cent in 1998.

Just how big is it?

Already, figures indicate massive growth underway in Europe's internet economy. According to the Gartner Group research firm it's growing by a whopping 87 per cent a year and should be worth $1.2 trillion by 2004. That's up from a mere $53 billion as of October 2000. (The internet economy is measured as the total value of hardware, telecommunications infrastructure, software, services and content providers.) The study says the UK, Germany, France and Italy have the fastest growing net economies.

'The fastest component of Europe's growth will be online transactions, amounting to a total of 1.1 billion in four years.'

Gartner Group

The UK situation

The UK is well positioned to share in that boom. With fierce competition among service providers, an increasing number of people are getting hooked on the internet. In fact the UK was the most connected country in Europe at the end of 2000 with 29.6 per cent of households accessing the internet, according to a report by research firm NetValue. There has been an explosion in internet-related business in the UK. There have been some high-profile failures as well, indicating that the market may have reached a new maturity, outgrowing its early rush-to-market stage.

NEW ECONOMY SNAPSHOT

UK consumers spent $750 million online last year, according to Jupiter Media Metrix.

The number of businesses who say they have plans to expand their web presence is growing. According to a recent report commissioned by the Department of Trade and Industry, 27 per cent of UK businesses now trade online, the same percentage as in the United States and Canada and a higher percentage than in Germany and Sweden. The survey also found that 34 per cent of UK companies get or make payments online from customers and suppliers, more than any other European country surveyed.

Observations on the New Economy

One of the most popular New Economy stereotypes is the get-rich-quick young dot com millionaire leading a life of glamour and excitement. In reality, people who work for dot coms and e-commerce companies will tell you it's mostly about dedication and hard work. But it is also about passion and excitement. Here are some observations from people working in the UK's New Economy concerning what they think the main differences are.

Johanna Walker, Head of Content and Commerce Operations, confetti.co.uk (*www.confetti.co.uk*): 'You're rarely a pioneer in the traditional industries unless you are a genius or very senior. At confetti **everyone has the chance to contribute** and make their mark at every level. I think the main thing to know is it is incredibly **hard work**. I once heard someone say the internet was the new rock'n'roll but frankly if you aren't too tired to schmooze in the West End after work you aren't doing something right. I gave up going to most dos and events when I started falling asleep in the wine.'

Adam Ellis, Head of Human Resources, Moonfruit.com (*www.moonfruit.com*): 'What differentiates our business from traditional companies is the **speed** at which things happen. **Change** is a major part of our daily lives and this can make some people who are used to a more traditional career path feel insecure. Belief in your own abilities, the business plan and your colleagues is the best way of getting through the uncertainties of a start-up but this requires teamwork and focus.'

Zoe Barnes, GoJobsite (*www.gojobsite.co.uk*): 'Jobsite is very different from traditional business because it is very **fast moving** and **dynamic**. Anything and everything is possible and we must all react to a wide variety of changes that occur every day.'

Rosie Reed, Editor, everywoman.co.uk (*www.everywoman.co.uk*): 'Our business is fundamentally no different from a traditional business except that we make decisions far quicker. As a site whose objective is to offer resources and information to our community, we see ourselves as being in the service industry. We do not think of ourselves as a "dot com" business per se, we are a company that just happens to conduct its business over the internet. Having said that, this industry moves **very quickly** and we need staff that can also do that.'

Mike With, Editor, Soccernet (*www.soccernet.com*): 'Differences are often hyped by people working online who want to think they are somehow special. Actually, they are just like everyone else. Yes, there are occasions when we can move more quickly than companies doing more traditional business, but there are also times when we get to sit and take stock. Maybe our **opportunities and vistas are a little broader** than some people's.'

Sridhar Gowda, co-founder, Countrybookshop.co.uk
(*www.countrybookshop.co.uk*): '[How are we different from a traditional business?] We *do* have a traditional business. Working for dot coms is **challenging** as the business models are constantly changing; **interesting** as there is so much development happening; **satisfying** as you can make your own rules. It's often remarked that these are exciting times and they are – but it's also been a lot of **hard work** and late nights!'

Sally Webster, Human Resources Director, bol.com
(*www.uk.bol.com*): 'I think the main difference is the **lack of formal hierarchy** in the organization. At bol.com all employees from the MD downwards sit in an open-plan, easy-access environment. The general way of working is much less formal and procedures are kept to a minimum. Business is conducted at a much **faster pace** than in traditional businesses, and there are **constant changes** both internally and in the marketplace. People coming into the sector need to understand that high energy and commitment are required at all levels.'

Katie Wells, UK Marketing Manager, Wideyes (*www.wideyes.co.uk*):
'[The differences with traditional industry are:] **Less structure, faster pace**, speed to market, **dependency on technology**, [you] learn quickly, room for opportunity and potential for self-fulfilment. The team tends to be young with a work-hard, play-hard mentality.'

Paul Basham, Chief Operating Officer, y-creds.co.uk (*www.y-creds.co.uk*): 'Different from a traditional company? In no way whatsoever. We have tight control over costs, we price our products to make a profit, we operate from an office **just like anyone else**. Our corporate culture is a little unusual but then each and every company is different in this regard!'

Annabel Roaf, Human Resources and Recruitment Manager, The First Resort (*www.thefirstresort.com*): 'The greatest difference would be the **speed** at which things progress and evolve. Timelines are hours, not days and weeks, not months. We are also more **creative** – we think of different and innovative ways of doing things. For someone joining a new dot com they must accept that processes and controls are still being established and not to expect the well-oiled machine that you may find in a large corporate environment. On an individual level, people must realize that whatever level they join at they will have an impact on the business – they are very visible. For most people this is great because you are so **close to the hub of the business**. It will not suit those who are happier hiding away and having little or no responsibility.'

Barb Upchurch, Editor, Loot.com (*www.loot.com*): 'Each department requires different skills, and many of them are not technical. For example, marketing the site is similar to marketing the paper, with the exception of the online marketing (banners, push mail, permission marketing, etc.). Because this area is relatively new, it is difficult to find employees with this skill, and things **change** *extremely* rapidly. We all learn together as the market changes.'

Alexandra Rowley, Gnash Communications, representing networking group First Tuesday (*www.firsttuesday.com*): 'It is generally a **high-risk** industry in comparison to the traditional economy. A regular income is not necessarily guaranteed, depending on how the dot com's first, second, and third round of funding develop as well as its marketing and audience success. It's also a **high-stress** environment with often massive amounts of stress and pressure. However, it is a **great environment for learning** and tearing away the constraints of a traditional career path, providing you have drive, ambition and belief in what you are doing.'

David Ferguson, Vice President of Products and Technology, Zeus Technology (*www.zeus.co.uk*): 'We **move extremely quickly** and we operate on much tighter schedules and we need to meet them. Our people are extremely committed to what we are doing. Someone coming in needs to understand that it's going to be **hard work**, that a lot is going to be expected of them, but if they can deliver, the **rewards** will be there for them. **Responsibility** is there for the taking, all you need to do is ask.'

David Gilroy, Operations Director, Sift (*www.sift.co.uk*): 'People need to understand the **pace** at which things in the dot com world happen. They have to be prepared to push the envelope and accept just when you've got something working, often as not you throw it away and start again. People need to understand the technology, but depending on the role they go into, they do not need to be able to "do it", e.g. an account manager or producer does not have to be the best HTML programmer, they just need to understand what it can do. So in this respect I think anyone that works in New Media needs to be able to program some HTML, even if they are in a sales role they need to understand how long things take [and] what's possible.'

Marcus Marcou, Managing Director, BusinessesForSale.com (*www.businessesforsale.com*): 'Traditional businesses have a chain of command in place. In an advertising agency it goes Group Account Director, Account Director, Senior Account Executive, Account Executive. And that's a creative industry. At a newspaper you have an editor, deputy editor, chief sub-editor, sub-editor, and that filters down across many different departments – Sport, News, etc. Start-ups and dot com start-ups have all the senior positions filled from the top – MD, Finance Director, Business Development Director, Marketing and Sales Director – but very little resource underneath. The traditional pyramid is replaced by a **flat structure**. As MD I see my role as "Primus Inter Pares" – First Among Equals. It's the nature of any start-up that has money. It also means that the senior brass make the tea, do the photocopies and collect the post. And that's fun too.'

Michael Smith, Chief Executive Officer, Firebox (*www.firebox.com*): '[There's a] very **laid-back** but **hard-working** atmosphere. The job is not just a job. It blurs the distinction between work and home life. There's relatively **little corporate structure** – it's very flexible, and much more of a meritocracy. It's a hell of a lot more fun!'

Norman Smith, Allcures.com (*www.allcures.com*): 'Essentially there is **nothing different**. All businesses, enterprises and organizations need the same enthusiasm and commitment to succeed.'

Rob Houghton, Managing Director, reallymoving.com (*www.reallymoving.com*): '[The differences with the off-line world include:] 1) **speed** of decision-making, 2) **lack of politics** with large organization (although there's always some); 3) **trust** is as important as legal agreements.'

Robert Leslie, Content Manager/Editor, Iglu.com (*www.iglu.com*): 'With the internet, there are **no boundaries** – [it] sounds like an old cliché but the same is true for the business models applied to the internet medium. We can conceivably achieve a lot more than our non-internet rivals and touch a limitless audience – it is just a case of making it happen. There is room for new and great ideas and this is not only the work of the hierarchy. Instead, our team spirit and **horizontal network hierarchy** allows anyone to conceive of and follow through on ideas.'

Serena Doshi, Managing Director, Liv4now.com (*www.liv4now.com*): 'We run our business with the same goals as a traditional one, focusing on growing the business model, driving steady growth on our path to profitability and providing added value to our users and clients. The major difference from traditional business is the **speed** at which things happen. **Flexibility** is a must and opportunities should be maximized at all times.'

Steve Chippington, Marketing Director, Shopsmart.com (*uk.shopsmart.com*): 'It should not be different. [A dot com company] has a product, it develops a brand, it has customers, it needs to build loyalty … but most of all it needs to have a clear plan, strong systems and make a profit. **Just like any other business**. The only real difference is **speed**. It's fast. And it does not suffer from the usual mid-management black hole, i.e. cultural changes only.'

Tim Levene, Director of Business Development, flutter.com (*www.flutter.com*): 'There are many areas where flutter.com differs from a traditional business, the most important ones (from an employee point of view) include: **personal ownership** of the success of the business; exceptional **pace** of development both personally and from a company perspective; impact on and access to the executive management team. Like any start-up business, commitment levels are very high and job responsibilities change rapidly. The nature of the dot com world means that there will always be people wanting to do what you do, so you must be better and improve continuously; having a good product now will not make it a good product in three months. This environment means that **flexibility** and **commitment** are key demands for anyone looking to join a dot com; you get to own and drive the success or failure of the company you join – but you must work for it.'

Katharin Strauss, Recruitment Manager, OneSwoop.com
(*www.oneswoop.com*): 'What most people like about working here is the **diversity** of the experience … They enjoy the exposure gained from working in cross-functional teams and expanding beyond the traditional boundaries of their job title. Conversely, it can be physically, mentally and emotionally **demanding** – at times even frustrating – to have to juggle many projects at the same time and to work with the uncertainty of constantly shifting priorities. The **speed of change** in a dot com business can be both exciting and demanding on its employees. While we have the thrill of working with a medium that allows you to implement new initiatives and therefore change your offering overnight, the fulfilment element of the business must be able to keep up with that pace … It is crucial to remain business-aware, see the impact of what is happening in your area across the rest of the company, and work closely with other departments to understand their needs. **Risk** is probably the most important differentiator. Most dot coms are secure only as long as their investors have faith in their ability to succeed, which means they will have key performance targets to achieve, often in incredibly short time frames. There is no doubt that this places added stress on employees and if an individual is risk-averse by nature they would probably not wish to put themselves through this! However, in many cases that risk can be outweighed by the potential reward – not only in terms of the equity they might earn in a growing young company, but in terms of the experience they will gain and the marketability of their skills even after a relatively short time spent working for a dot com.'

Kelly Wilkins, Human Resources Officer, fish4.co.uk
(*www.jobs.fish4.co.uk*): 'The only real difference in working in a dot com is that it is a **fast-paced** industry and you need to react to changes in the market quickly and effectively.'

Roy Bliss, Chief Operating Officer, Talkcast (*www.talkcast.com*): 'The company differs from others that I have worked in by dint of **all employees being shareholders** or option holders – everyone. They are all stake holders and want to make the business a success. None of us do this for our health – it is because we want to drive value to each other and to investors in the form of share valuation, etc. It may also be that someone enjoys the environment that we portray – open plan, **fun**, **vibrant** and **open communication**.'

the new world

from here to e

momentum

the skills shortage

- ◆ The New Economy's evolution

- ◆ Shifting sands

NEW ECONOMY SNAPSHOT

Employees from nearly one-third of US companies have left to work for a dot com, according to company Management Recruiters International.

One of the most exciting things about the New Economy is that there are very few people around with the skill sets and years of experience on the job, because it's so new. The skills shortage – especially in core-IT functions – has been a characteristic of the job market for the past decade. The growth of the personal computer market already required

---

NEW ECONOMY SNAPSHOT

A November 1999 study by Forrester Research said 90 per cent of European IT companies are suffering from a skills shortage and two-thirds experience delay on projects or problems with delivery as a result.

burgeoning numbers of staff. Now, the growing popularity of e-commerce has exacerbated the situation. That's affecting not just pure internet programming areas, but any company hoping to stake out an e-commerce presence. As each new strand of technology is developed, up goes the number of people not just to maintain it but develop it and adapt its uses.

NEW ECONOMY SNAPSHOT

The speed at which e-business is evolving is having an unprecedented impact on staffing levels within companies. A report by PricewaterhouseCoopers' Global Technology Industry Group estimated that e-business staffing will rise from 15 per cent in 1999 to 28 per cent in 2002 with 'New Entrants' (new companies) predicting the highest percentage of e-business staff. It said that as a by-product of e-business growth, many companies and in particular the 'New Entrants' are outsourcing many of the support processes, allowing management to focus on core business functions.

According to a recent report by Andersen Consulting, internet-related employment in the UK will more than double in the next two years, leading to 80,000 vacancies by 2003. It says the number of web-based jobs in existing dot coms and existing companies will reach 852,000 by 2002, compared with 307,000 in 1999. The report found that 88 per cent of the 160 organizations interviewed said there are not enough suitably qualified people to work on internet projects.

NEW ECONOMY SNAPSHOT

By 2002 the internet economy will employ more than 10 million people across a variety of industries in the USA, the five largest European economies and Ireland, according to Andersen Consulting. At least 3 million of those jobs will be in Europe. The internet sector will be worth $597 billion in the European countries.

Finding and retaining staff is the single most important issue facing the technology industry, according to a PricewaterhouseCoopers study released in March 2000. Of almost 300 companies surveyed, it found that 70 per cent had severe difficulties hiring qualified staff, not just in strictly technical areas but all across the board, including people with e-commerce skills.

As of the end of 2000, there were approximately 1.2 million unfilled IT jobs in Western Europe, 220,468 of those in the UK alone, according to International Data Corporation. IDC says if the current trend continues there could be as many as 1.7 million unfilled jobs in Europe's technology sector in the next three years – a 13 per cent shortage overall.

Western Europe stands to lose £380 billion between 2000 and 2003 in lost productivity and tax revenues, according to recent research by Datamonitor. PricewaterhouseCoopers' study says the talent dearth has held down growth rates by about half, and that the trend will worsen as businesses look to add up to 30 per cent more staff to e-business-related activity.

NEW ECONOMY SNAPSHOT

Virtually all the US jobs lost in the production or distribution of goods between 1969 and 1995 have been replaced by office jobs.

As e-commerce begins to be standard practice among enterprises, replacing or complementing old sales and marketing practices, old skill sets will become redundant and growth will happen in IT-related skills. Of course, core-IT jobs already require high levels of specialized knowledge. However, many jobs will require more general computer skills and knowledge. Overall, says a recent report by Datamonitor, 'Future jobs which are created will be higher-skilled and higher-paying that those that will be displaced.'

Said Steve Freeman, partner, Andersen Consulting, 'The good news is that the internet is creating more jobs than it is destroying, even when you look at traditional business models. And this peripheral job creation is likely to be significant in the short term as established businesses invest in building up new internet operations alongside their existing businesses.'

A recent report by IDC agreed, saying, 'Essentially there is rapid growth in demand for personnel who can complement some general technical knowledge with business knowledge and skills.'

The New Economy's evolution

The internet economy had its first major shakedown starting in April 2000, when there was a massive 'correction' in the technology stock market. Before then, a dizzying number of companies had rushed to be first to market, especially in the business-to-consumer (b2c) category. During the gold rush speculation was rife, and millions were made, primarily in stock options. Eventually sober second thoughts began to emerge, especially as investors, who had helped fuel the boom, began to demand that companies turn a profit. Suddenly companies had to compete for venture capital; the smaller and weaker started to fold.

Shifting sands

But it would be a mistake to think that these often high-profile and expensive failures mean the experiment is over. The internet has already revolutionized business and will continue to do so in fundamental ways. But the market has matured. What that means for prospective employees is that it is now critical to identify which sectors are solid and showing growth. As of this writing the hot areas are wireless, peer-to-peer networking and the business-to-business retail sector. 'Only the strongest will survive the b2c shakedown,' said John A. Challenger, Chief Executive Officer of international outplacement firm Challenger, Gray & Christmas, and those firms will also prosper as consumers find it easier to identify with the long-lasting brands. 'Heading every dot com CEO's priority list is the need to generate enough paying customers to hit critical mass. Both investor and employee concerns are centred on "turning the corner" – reaching a point when the business turns profitable. Many of these new companies will fail and disappear. Some will be acquired by traditional companies hoping to integrate an e-commerce presence quickly into their current operations. Others will be purchased by leading companies hoping to build enough revenue to get over the hump.' (More on e-commerce trends in Chapter 13.)

NEW ECONOMY SNAPSHOT

The shakedown in the US online services and retail sector led to thousands of job losses at dot coms during 2000. Challenger, Gray & Christmas said 22,267 dot com job cuts were announced between December 1999, when the firm began tracking such data, and October 2000. The study showed that 44, or 16 per cent, of 274 US dot com companies failed in the same period. Services, such as consulting, financial and information, suffered the most cuts, accounting for 36 per cent or 8113. Retail was second with 5450 cuts. Health and fitness jumped from fifth in September to third in October with 2190. Teen and related sites suddenly surfaced in October with 328 cuts or six per cent of the monthly total.

All this should serve as a serious warning to prospective employees – it's critical in such a volatile market to pick a company with a solid management team and secure funding. Also, would-be workers should learn to consider a company's failure as a learning opportunity. People who have lost jobs in the e-tailing sectors are still hot commodities as the bigger companies consolidate (see Chapter 16). And they're moving on more of their own accord as well. Turnover rates in high-tech and the New Economy generally are way above the national average – in the USA the average employee leaves in 13 months, a trend which has been noted in the UK as well. Employee loyalty is eroding among all demographic groups. New Economy workers have to learn to embrace the revolving door. (More in Chapter 14.)

NEW ECONOMY SNAPSHOT

A Datamonitor report found that 68 per cent of small and medium enterprises in Western Europe reported that company growth is being hindered by an acute shortage of skilled IT workers.

the new world

from here to e

momentum

part two
the skills you need

chapter three
getting started

what you need in your new economy toolbox

- A quick mind
- Computer/web skills
- Technology literacy
- E-commerce
- Speed
- Visionary skills
- Flexibility
- Multiskills
- Team skills
- Self-motivation
- Risk taking
- Streamlining
- What New Economy employers want

Here's a short list of the skills you'll need in the New Economy. In later chapters we'll look at where you go to get them as quickly and efficiently as possible.

- **A quick mind:** In the past, workers needed to be skilled with their hands. In the knowledge and information-based New Economy, being smart counts. Many of the new jobs are professional, managerial or technical in nature. Qualifications and levels of education are important.

- **Computer/web skills:** Not long ago it was possible to work for a company that used computers and not need to know much more than how to turn it on and blunder about with a bit of basic wordprocessing. These days everyone needs to know at least the basics of how to use office software packages. If you are in a dot com you need to know a lot more then just how to surf the web and send e-mail.

- **Technology literacy:** In traditional industry, knowing your market is important, as is keeping abreast of developments that might change your product or your production line. In a dot com, it's essential that you know what's going on in the world of technology so you can incorporate the latest technology into your environment. For business development, you need to know what nascent technologies might become important. Learn to forecast. If you wait around to see what actually works, your competitors may have beaten you to the punch.

- **E-commerce:** It's essential to learn about the special rules that govern the world of electronic commerce. The fact that commercial transactions can now be performed electronically rather than face to face or over the phone has big implications for all businesses, not just dot coms. The web offers customers shopping opportunities 24/7 and an endless amount of information. As a company your shop is on every single high street in the world. But so is everyone else's. How do you stand out and engage the customer? Tailor your pitch to a highly specific group of customers? People are only beginning to figure out what to do with the mountains of data they can now track about their customers.

- **Speed:** Learn to operate in internet time. As mentioned, the internet's conventional wisdom is that a year in internet time equals a quarter of a year in real time. That means you can't always wait for the right answer or business model to present itself – decisions often must be made in the dark or on gut instinct. Learning to set priorities is critical. Any decision is better than none at all in the world of the web.

- **Visionary skills:** Be passionate about your career and product, even if you are just starting out. In a workforce without a lot of experience, enthusiasm is a must. Set big goals and smaller ones, targets and timetables, for both yourself and your business. Make sure everyone knows what they are. Review them often and discard as necessary.

- ◆ **Flexibility:** Once you've taken a decision you must be able to discard it just as quickly if it's not producing the desired result. A company's creative destruction rate, its ability to shed old practices while embracing the new, is critical to its survival. Apply that lesson to your own career. Being adaptable is perhaps the most important character trait you should possess.

- ◆ **Multiskills:** You should develop an insatiable appetite for acquiring new skills, which is critical as we move away from a jobs-for-life world. Successful New Economy people may not be the ones who are most qualified, but the ones prepared to work the hardest to become that way on any particular project. Turn every job into a learning opportunity.

- ◆ **Team skills:** Know how to be a team player and how to adapt to the prevailing culture on a given project. Take responsibility for your area, assist others and don't tread on others' territories or undermine their work. The internet economy is all about networking, and more so than in traditional industry, what goes around comes around. Don't cross members of your own team. If word of mouth has it that you are not 'a good cultural fit' you won't be hired.

- ◆ **Self-motivation:** Learn to be your own manager. In the dot com world there's often no one looking over your shoulder – no one has time. That means you can have plenty of freedom, but plenty of responsibility. If you're not used to being unsupervised, you may need to learn a few management skills and apply them to yourself. Learn to set your own priorities.

- ◆ **Risk taking:** If you're currently working in an organization that doesn't encourage creativity and risk-taking it can be stultifying and frustrating, making even the most creative and enthusiastic employee bitter and complacent. Learn to peel back those layers and take risks again, by generating and proposing new ideas. If they are accepted, take responsibility for following them through.

- ◆ **Streamlining:** Practise ruthless efficiency in the way you structure tasks and teams. Don't let your organization get bogged down in layers that are unproductive – in the internet world there is no time to waste – yours or your employees.

What New Economy employers want

But you don't have to take my word for it. Dozens of dot com and e-commerce companies were interviewed for this book and asked for their top three criteria. There was a remarkable convergence of opinion on what they want. Only a few people reported that actual dot com experience was required before they would consider hiring an employee. Of course, in most senior positions, experience is required. But for the most part managing directors, chief executive officers and human resources directors said that **enthusiasm**, **flexibility** and **having the right attitude** are the key attributes they are looking for.

Marcus Marcou is Managing Director of BusinessesForSale.com (*www.businessesforsale.com*) which brings together buyers and sellers of businesses. He put it succinctly from an employer's point of view. 'The qualities you need are **flexibility**, **an open mind**, the ability to not only throw textbooks out of the window but to realize that what you are doing is writing the next textbook. No idea is original. The deal here is **can you rework the old ideas?** We're making the wheel faster – not reinventing it. It means the best ideas are still very simple. I'm looking for people who intuitively get that. I'm looking for **intuitive people**. People in touch with their gut. **People who aren't afraid to take a risk**. There are no models to go with. I'm looking for people who are not afraid to fail. It's more important than anything else to me because that informs how creative you can be.'

Sally Webster, Human Resources Director at major book and music retailer bol.com (*www.uk.bol.com*), says the rapid change of pace makes **flexibility** critical in her office. 'Obviously it helps if prospective employees are **"internet savvy"** and although they may not have worked in New Media before, they need to demonstrate a knowledge of, and passion for the medium. Over and above that they need to be **flexible** and comfortable working at a **blistering pace**, in an environment where the only certainty is change. **Creativity** is also important and **the ability to solve problems** and circumvent obstacles quickly. Finally, **team players** are required. There are so many critical dependencies within the business that there's no room for prima donnas or empire builders. This sector is best suited to those who are genuinely **inspired** by the opportunity to contribute something unique to our medium, and will **roll their sleeves up** and get stuck in.'

Employees need to have a flexible attitude first and foremost, agrees Rosie Reed, Editor of major women's portal everywoman.co.uk (*www.everywoman.co.uk*). 'We need staff that recognize that this is not a 9 to 5 job and we require **flexibility** in both the time they put in and the jobs they do during their working day. While everyone has a job description, we sometimes require "all hands on deck" … Depending on the job, we don't require a high level of technical know-how, but we do require **basic PC skills** and a **good understanding of the internet**. **Communication skills** are a must, experience is preferred but "dot com experience" not a prerequisite. **Enthusiasm** is a must, **creativity** is preferred and a lot of **energy**.'

Katie Wells, UK Marketing Manager for Wideyes (*www.Wideyes.co.uk*), a web-based recruitment company, agreed. 'Number one is **flexibility**. Change is constant in this industry. The ability to adjust constantly and be able to work effectively in a changing environment is fundamental. Number two is **tenacity**. There can be a lot of ups and downs working for a dot com. Quick recovery from testing times is important if objectives are to be met. Number three is **enthusiasm**.'

Katharin Strauss, Recruitment Manager for online car-buying portal OneSwoop (*www.oneswoop.com*), placed **flexibility** and **adaptability** after experience. 'Our working environment is incredibly fast paced and often ambiguous. Individuals who join our team are frequently stretched outside their "normal" remit and will be asked to take on tasks for which they may have little or no experience because of the pace of the business and the need to keep ahead of the competition.' Her third criterion is the ability of an employee to **take ownership** of their role in the team. 'As a business we have an enormous amount to achieve in a short time frame. If one person at any level within the company lets the team down, we all lose out. Our employees will have the opportunity to own a piece of the business so it is in their own interest to put in 100 per cent and strive to do their job that bit better.'

Having dollops of enthusiasm is high on Mel Garfield's list. He represents ihavemoved.com (*www.ihavemoved.com*), a company that lets people know you've moved house. 'The most important thing is that candidates are **enthusiastic**. I need to see them spark about ihavemoved.com. It doesn't necessarily have to be about the service itself – it can be about the environment, the perks, the location, the industry – but I want to see them respond positively to what I tell them about the company or elements of it. Candidates also need to have excellent **communication skills** and to be well researched and **analytical** in their thought process … In terms of their **character**, I would say they need to be able to think on their feet, respond quickly and thrive on challenges.'

'It depends on the specific position, but **enthusiasm** is probably the most important quality,' said Michael Smith, CEO and co-founder of Firebox (*www.firebox.com*), which specializes in gifts for men. 'Someone who really wants to join our company is very valuable. This is far more valuable than experience. It is easy to spot these people in interviews. Anyone who spends time before the first interview researching our company and has suggestions on how we can improve our site is in a great position. One guy came to his interview with a 15-page report on site improvements. I was ready to hire him on the spot. **Character** is important. They must fit in with our existing culture. **Real-world intelligence** is important as well. Anyone who is smart and enthusiastic can learn just about anything in a few weeks so it wouldn't worry me that they came from a completely different background.'

Owen Tyzack, with e-procurement website buyingteam (*www.buyingteam.com*), agrees that enthusiasm counts. 'For some of the more basic roles, **enthusiasm**, **creativity** and **common sense** will provide the candidate with the necessary tools to adjust to a fast-paced environment with a steep learning curve. As with any career, a genuine **interest** is always necessary and in many cases an interest in the **internet/e-commerce** will often carry a certain amount of technical expertise. The more IT-orientated roles are often highly technical and will require some form of previous experience or academic grounding to secure a candidacy. It is important for a candidate to have a general overview of how the industry works, how money is generated through affiliate deals and advertising and to become familiar with how e-commerce affects both the b2b and b2c markets.'

Glenn Elliot is with unified communications company YAC.com (*www.yac.com*). 'The main thing we are looking for in any employee is a good **attitude** – self starters with a **"can do"** outlook on work. This means **enthusiasm** and **team spirit**. In terms of experience, most skills in terms of marketing are transferable from industry to industry but if we can find people with an IT or internet background, it is obviously an advantage. Everyone has to be willing to learn very quickly.'

Enthusiasm and potential are everything, says Human Resources and Recruitment Manager Annabel Roaf with online travel agent The First Resort (*www.thefirstresort.com*). 'For more junior positions we are happy to take on people who we consider to have **genuine enthusiasm** for the position and can demonstrate true **potential**. They must be able to demonstrate that they are **internet savvy**; this falls into two areas – the technical and the commercial. It is important that they have an understanding of behind the scenes (have they at least heard of HTML?). There is so much information available to them and they will have a good head start if they have some **background knowledge** (even if they've never actually put it into practice). I think it is equally, or even more important for them to have a good grasp of **e-commerce**. For example, how does the internet interact with business? What are the commercial implications behind a dot com?'

Bill Wright, Business Development Manager for European business-to-business e-commerce site for the building industry BuildOnline (*www.buildonline.com*), says **experience** is the most important characteristic but second in line is **cultural fit**. 'Successful candidates are those who display a high level of **enthusiasm**, **creativity** and **quick thinking** which fits in with the general culture of the company. The work hard/play hard ethic is very much a part of our organization and individuals who are interested in owning responsibility and stretching themselves to achieve are well recognized and encouraged to grow.' He also cites **flexibility** as important. 'As a dynamic company in a relatively new industry, we look to employ staff who are able to work within a moving, fluid environment and who are able to focus on a range of tasks and responsibilities that may not fit into their realm of experience or original job specification.'

Enthusiasm, **experience** and **character** are the qualities sought above all by Goodmigrations.co.uk (*www.goodmigrations.co.uk*), a portal for people moving home, according to researcher Adrian Smith. He says IT positions require technical know-how, but there are no special skills required for non-IT positions. 'General principles of the business are the same as for traditional companies, just faster.'

Norman Smith, with online pharmacy and health website Allcures.com (*www.allcures.com*), says simply, 'Enthusiasm, commitment and communication skills.'

Character tops COO Paul Basham's list. His company y-creds.co.uk (*www.y-creds.co.uk*) is an e-commerce site catering to teenagers. 'Criterion number one is strength of **character** – tenacity and an ability to still perform in the face of adversity. We prefer people with some professional training, for example lawyers, accountants for senior management, and everyone *must* have a sense of **humour**! Acceptance of **flexible** working practices is essential. You may be needed on a weekend or at 11pm on a Friday, but if you want to take a day off here or there to run your life then we are flexible. Finally, an **inquisitive nature** is a plus.'

Character tops the list for Zoe Barnes, who works at the popular online job listing website GoJobsite (*www.gojobsite.co.uk*). Her rankings were **character**, **communication skills** followed by **enthusiasm**. 'For someone in marketing and customer support we look for people who have thorough **knowledge of the internet**. When we are recruiting sales people, they don't necessarily need technical knowledge but we look for people who are **able to quickly learn** the product and have the ability to **clearly explain** it over the phone … As a general comment, everyone we interview for any position must have excellent **communication skills** and must demonstrate the desire to be part of a **team**.'

Roy Bliss, Chief Operating Officer for Talkcast (*www.talkcast.com*), the wireless and telecommunications company, says character counts. 'Obviously each role will be defined by certain characteristics like experience and technical understanding, but those functions are defined by the role. Perhaps the best way to answer your question is to look at the general theme we seek in our employees – essentially that revolves around **character** and **style**. The company is still relatively young – being about 15 months old – and employs north of 130 people. But the consistent theme is **personality**.'

Steve Chippington is Marketing Director of Shopsmart (*uk.shopsmart.com*), an online price comparison service that lets consumers compare the prices offered by retailers on a range of products. 'My criteria start with **personality** – it's the most important of all. They need to fit into the team and have the right **attitudes**.

After that I want to know that they are **classically trained** in marketing (ideally fast-moving consumer goods) and have the ability to **see things through**, working within a **flexible team structure**. Finally, I want to see the **passion** to get into the industry and the hunger to work really hard in a new arena. They should not be afraid of the unknown, and [should also be] happy to work from a blank sheet of paper [and] take **ownership**. People need to be prepared to move back and feel secure in the fact that they are moving into a New World with a new language and new parameters.'

Tony Smith, Managing Editor with online IT news website The Register (*www.theregister.co.uk*), says personality and a familiarity with the beat matter over technical proficiency, especially in content jobs. 'Generally I'm looking for **enthusiasm** and **competence** above all other criteria. Competence is really just an amalgamation of **know-how** and **experience** … that depends on the job and on the nature of the company. I'd expect candidates to **know what the web is** and broadly how it works, but if I'm recruiting a journalist, say, I'd be more interested in their **knowledge of the subject** matter than their knowledge of the net.'

Rob Houghton, founder and Managing Director of moving-home services website reallymoving.com (*www.reallymoving.com*), says attitude is everything. 'My employee criteria are **attitude** (open, non-judgemental, hardworking); **personality** (fit with team, finds work fun); **technical/commercial experience** relevant to specific role.'

Having a positive outlook ranked as number one for Serena Doshi, Managing Director of Liv4now.com (*www.liv4now.com*), a lifestyle channel for 18–34 year-olds. 'Although proven experience in the specific area is very important, we like looking for "do-ers" – people who if they don't have the exact specific experience, have the **desire and personality** to learn and the **eagerness and skill** to be responsible enough to develop their own areas. **Creativity, innovation** and **dedication** count for a lot in this industry – qualifications are important but they are not the be-all and end-all.'

Tim Levene, Business Development Director at the UK's leading person-to-person betting site flutter.com (*www.flutter.com*), with a staff of 90, agrees passion matters. 'The specific requirements will vary with each role, for example a designer will have creativity valued more highly than a systems administrator, and we expect people to have the technical ability to fulfil their jobs. The common thread, however, for flutter.com is a **passion** for our business and their own job; we look to hire people based on their **talents**, these being **striving**, **thinking** and **relating**. People who have the technical ability but not the above will not be as successful in driving flutter.com forward.'

Being a **self-starter** is the most important factor for Johanna Walker, Head of Content and Commerce Operations at major UK wedding portal confetti.co.uk (*www.confetti.co.uk*). '**Motivation** is the crucial factor! In a flexible and non-hierarchical environment where everybody brings something unique to the party there is no room for people who have to be constantly monitored and coaxed. The **desire and ability to learn** are also paramount. I'd rather work with someone who started knowing some basic HTML but learnt Flash, Dreamweaver and Photoshop in the next six months than someone who came with great JavaScript and never progressed from there. **Creativity** is also key. Most of the questions you ask in this business don't have set answers. You need to be able to both ask the right question and come up with a great solution.'

Alexandra Rowley, Gnash Communications, representing networking group First Tuesday (*www.firsttuesday.com*), agreed that employees need to be motivated. Her rankings were '1) drive/dedication, 2) ability to think on their feet and learn quickly, 3) experience that can be translated into the New Economy – not necessarily specific New Economy experience.'

Robert Leslie, Content Manager/Editor with online ski holiday bookers Iglu.com (*www.iglu.com*), agrees that an understanding of e-commerce is necessary. 'For any position a certain understanding of the **web/business** is needed – **creativity** and **dedication** are the key. There may be long hours and hard work, so **real interest** and **enthusiasm** shine through.'

Talent counts whereas skills can be taught, says Adam Ellis, Head of Human Resources for Moonfruit.com (*www.moonfruit.com*), an online website-building community with its own web-building software. 'The important point to remember is that you can always train a skill deficiency, you cannot train talent. Moonfruit assesses candidates against a vacant role on their **talents first**: these primarily are based around the individual's **approach to work**, **creativity** and **enthusiasm**, but include **diligence**, **discipline**, **customer-facing skills** and the **desire to achieve**. The more junior the position the more you are assessing someone on **talent**. Middle to senior management positions require a mix of talent and experience in order for the candidate to do the job successfully. Depending on the role, either the skills or the talents will be dominant but never at the expense of the other. Artists and creatives are more talent-focused jobs but individuals still require skills in order to execute their ideas.'

Margaret Amein, Managing Director of home improvement site Improveline.com (*www.improveline.com*), says being smart counts. Her top picks were **intelligence** followed by experience in applying a **structured approach** to problems and projects, to both solve and prevent problems, with a very commercial and common-sense approach. 'You will need to react quickly in completely new situations. [You] must be able to do many different tasks at once rather than just one thing.' **Project management skills** and strong **analytical skills** were also critical. 'No one knows the answers in many areas of the e-world so we need people who can analyze the data to chart out the best direction.'

Said David Ferguson, Vice President of Products and Technology, Zeus Technology (*www.zeus.co.uk*), a web-server software company, 'Number one is **ability**. How ability is measured varies from group to group inside the company. We don't measure raw IQ, but for example, for a software engineer, it's crucial that they understand and know how to apply the principles of software engineering and be capable of writing good software efficiently. Number two is **fit**. There are certain key characteristics of Zeus employees – **enthusiasm**, we're not interested in a "can do" attitude, we need a **"will do" attitude**. We're also looking for **openness to new ideas**, the ability to adapt past experience to our way of doing things, openness and honesty, and the desire to see the company succeed. Number three is **experience**. Experience is important in a number of ways. Firstly, it justifies the candidate's salary expectations. Secondly, it minimizes the delay between starting work and coming up to speed. Thirdly, obtaining feedback on our internal performance is key to managing our growth. It's great to bring people on board who have worked in at least of couple of different companies who can then adapt their experiences to our way of doing things and thereby improve our effectiveness.'

Jennifer Burt is the Editor of babyworld (*www.babyworld.co.uk*), part of icircle, the women's channel. She says traditional industry experience counts in the online word. Her top three criteria: 'Publishing **experience of any kind**: newspapers/magazines/books/online; Good **communication skills** as employees have to represent the company; and an in**terest** in the subject matter (in our case, parenting). We update constantly so deadlines, rather than completing a project in a month's time, are set as soon as you can do it. You need to be **flexible, adaptable** (which doesn't mean being available 24 hours, more that you need to be able to **prioritize** work) and **thrive on change** rather than routine.'

Barb Upchurch, Editor at online classifieds site Loot.com (*www.loot.com*), agrees that previous experience in a traditional company can be transferred. 'We started with the paper product, and many people who work here started with **no dot com experience**, as they have come from the paper, myself included!'

Mike With, Editor of leading online football site Soccernet (*www.soccernet.com*), agrees that traditional industry skills can be applied to content sites. He ranks knowledge of and **passion** for the subject first: 'It's no good working on a football website if you don't love the game and know how and why other people share that passion', followed by **demonstrable skills**, which could be through qualifications or experience, not necessarily online. 'You are plunged in at the deep end here and you have to know how to swim.' That's followed by '**energy** a.k.a. **enthusiasm, commitment**. No interest in having a regular social life is a distinct advantage!'

Sridhar Gowda co-founded book e-tailer Countrybookshop.co.uk (*www.countrybookshop.co.uk*). For design jobs he ranked **creativity**, **enthusiasm** and **communication** skills as his most desired skill set. For programming jobs, the top skills were **technical know-how**, **enthusiasm** and **team spirit**. 'Even though we are not looking for experts we do want them to have the fundamental knowledge of a programming language and an understanding of databases and have logical thinking and self learning capability,' he said.

David Gilroy, Operations Director with online b2b marketplace Sift (*www.sift.co.uk*), ranked the range of skills his company needs as follows: 'Sales – experience, tenacity, robust attitude. Design – creativity, listening skills, design skills. Technical – technical skill, work ethic, listening skills. Editors – writing skills, industry knowledge, networking skills. Business – all-round skills really.'

Sean Whyte, of brand new start-up Mentor (*www.seanwhyte.com*): 'We are about to employ our first person. We will be looking for tons of **enthusiasm, determination, passion** for the subject and technical skills in abundance. Internet companies tend (need) to be very fast moving and require people to be flexible. We rarely, if ever, meet or talk to our customers – a very big difference to a traditional business. People need to demonstrate an interest in the business concerned, have done their homework, and understand that it is not a route to sudden riches.'

chapter four
a good hard look

- ◆ Attitude

- ◆ Computer skills

- ◆ Internet skills

- ◆ Business knowledge

- ◆ Education

- ◆ Work experience

There are a range of skills necessary to survive and prosper in the New Economy: an understanding of technology, familiarity with e-commerce basics, mastering computer skills. But many of the basics you'll need are the same as in the traditional work world: a **good attitude**, **ambition** and **determination**. Not all of us sit down and plan our careers as comprehensively as we should – often it's just not a priority at the end of a long day or a very busy week. But before embarking on a big change, it's critical to set aside a few hours to look at where you've been, and come up with a vision of where you want to be.

Coming up with a plan will save you time and energy and give you a sense of purpose to propel you towards your goals. Attaining skills requires work, but it's much easier to do once you've identified your weak spots and set yourself a series of goals that are specific and attainable. Learning to take control of change is an increasingly critical skill in the work world these days. It's also a life skill you can use to help you cope with a world that just isn't going to slow down.

The following survey will help you identify your weaknesses comprehensively. Be brutally honest – you won't be able to move forward unless you do. If you are unsure of how to rate yourself in a particular catagory, ask an objective observer, perhaps someone you work with or an old friend. In some ways this is a wish list. But it's also a checklist. As you work through each section a clear picture will emerge of your strengths and weaknesses. In the next chapter we'll prioritize and focus your efforts.

Attitude

◆ Do you feel positive about the future?

◆ Can you bring enthusiasm to your workplace?

◆ Do you feel proactive, with the willpower and energy to effect change?

◆ Are you confident about speaking your mind?

◆ Do you have determination and drive?

◆ Are you hardworking and self-motivated?

◆ Do you have a flexible and creative approach to problem solving?

◆ Can you set priorities and change them quickly?

◆ Are you decisive?

◆ Do you treat mistakes as learning opportunities?

◆ Are you physically healthy?

◆ Can you handle stress effectively?

Computer skills

◆ Are you comfortable with the basics of computers? PC and Mac?

◆ Can you use basic office software for wordprocessing, spreadsheets, basic desktop publishing and slide-show presentations?

◆ Have you ever worked in a networked environment – a system where computers are interconnected and files may be shared?

Internet skills

◆ How knowledgeable are you about cyberspace? Do you have a good sense of what's available online and what the most popular sites are?

◆ Do you know what the leading UK offerings in cyberspace are?

◆ Do you use e-mail?

◆ Have you chatted online, posted to a message or bulletin board or subscribed to a mailing list or newsgroup?

◆ Have you downloaded or uploaded files?

◆ Have you explored video and audio on the web?

◆ Have you played online games?

◆ Have you made a website? If so, did you use authoring software or raw HTML?

◆ What software packages are you familiar with (e.g. Adobe Photoshop, Dreamweaver, Macromedia Flash)?

Business knowledge

◆ How much do you know about the company you work for?

◆ How much do you know about your industry in the UK and across Europe?

◆ Are you familiar with basic business principles?

◆ How often do you read books and magazines related to your industry?

◆ Do you have solid contacts?

Education

◆ What level of education did you attain?

◆ Have you taken additional courses relevant to your profession?

◆ Do you belong to professional organizations?

Work experience

◆ What positions have you held? For how long?

◆ Have you been in a leadership situation? Do you know how to motivate staff and harness their energy?

◆ Have you worked on a special project as part of a team?

◆ What kind of presentation skills do you have? Have you used them in a work setting?

◆ Do you have references?

◆ What kind of on-the-job training did you get or ask for?

◆ What kind of work goals have you set for yourself? Have you achieved them and if so how?

◆ Have you developed a network of contacts in and outside your company?

◆ Have you mentored a junior employee or been mentored?

◆ Are you able to strategize and build allies to attain your goals?

chapter five
fill in the blanks

- ◆ Attitude

- ◆ Computer skills

- ◆ Internet skills

- ◆ Business knowledge

- ◆ Education

- ◆ Work experience

Your ultimate goal is to acquire all the skills mentioned in Chapter 4's survey, not all at once, but over time. Now that you've done an inventory, check which areas need the most work. Where are your skills critically lacking? The sections below should help you set priorities, if you're not sure what requirements are the most important to employers.

Then set yourself a schedule for acquiring those goals. Decide which you need to work on right away, then look ahead, past your next job, and set skilling-up goals that will prepare you for the job after that one. Print out your survey answers – **your New Economy checklist** – and tape it somewhere prominent so you have a daily reminder of your goals. As you work your way through them, you'll feel a sense of accomplishment as you chart your progress.

Attitude

Having the right attitude is critical to the job. You can gloss over weaknesses in plenty of areas, but if a prospective employer senses your attitude is poor, you simply won't get the job. Developing a positive, enthusiastic outlook requires some mental work. But, like any other skill, it just takes practice. There's a lot of literature on the subject, and it's not this book's purpose to add to that, except to say that you should sample opinion widely to come up with what works for you. Draw on your personal support network of friends and family. Consider short courses for some specific areas such as leadership and presentation skills. Greater knowledge also leads to confidence, as does experience. Developing good work habits is the key to being effective. More on this in Chapter 6.

Computer skills

Computer skills are something you must have if you don't already. The best way to advance your understanding is to buy a computer complete with basic software. It is possible to access the internet through your television but since the vast majority of web work is currently geared to the PC environment your best bet is to invest where the majority is. Once you've got the kit, read the manual and use it. More on advancing your computer skills in Chapters 10 and 11. If you're interested in what mobile technology has to offer, such as accessing the internet over your mobile phone, it's wise to buy a package offering this as well and explore the options.

Internet skills

Internet access is getting cheaper all the time as competition by service providers heats up. If you can't afford your own computer, go to a cybercafé where you pay a fee to use one that's already connected. These are springing up everywhere, primarily as a way for people to check e-mail. Spend some time using the various search engines and learn how to work newsgroups. Try everything listed in Chapter 4's list of skills to acquire. Read magazines that cover the internet. Most of the newspapers have weekly columns on the web, and cyberspace itself is packed with sites that talk about what the hottest new thing is. For more resources on what's available on the net, check Chapter 10 and Appendix 1. With enough reading, you will begin to understand some of the technology behind the applications. On the net, what we can deliver is determined by how we can deliver it. More on technology in Chapter 11.

Business knowledge

Basic business skills can be learned in a formal setting by taking courses or, more typically, on the job by keeping your eyes and ears open and asking a lot of questions. There are many books and periodicals that deal with e-business (see Appendix 1). Use them to get acquainted with conventional wisdom in your area. More on this in Chapter 13.

Education

In a knowledge-based economy, learning is a part of life, not something you do in one go and put behind you. For entry-level jobs your formal education level is probably not critical, provided you are a graduate. But if you aspire to upper-level jobs you may need to enrol in a university course. Not all e-commerce jobs require MBAs but most top-level people will have one. Top core-IT jobs require high levels of qualifications. For specific skills, consider taking courses outside your working hours or by correspondence. More on that in Chapter 12.

Work experience

Establishing your work track record takes planning and hard work, but by focusing your efforts towards certain goals you can get there with a minimum of fuss. The skills that will look best on a résumé are fairly obvious: project leadership, team player, presentation and performance skills, and evidence of setting and achieving goals for the company. If you're not currently working towards these areas, you should be. More on how in Chapters 6 and 14.

chapter six
put your best face forward

- The skills you already have

- Skilling up

The skills you already have

In addition to acquiring the skills you don't already have, it's important to assess the transferable skills you've already acquired in traditional industry and play those to your advantage, both on your CV and in your interviews. Since so few people have the exact qualifications that dot coms and e-commerce operations need, employers take a close look at the traditional work experience acquired by their prospective employees. But what specific old-school work skills should you stress? Start by answering the following questions.

Have you ever:

- worked successfully as part of a team, and on your own?

- worked across boundaries and departments?

- worked on a project from start to finish?

- showed initiative?

- come up with a creative solution to a difficult problem?

- encountered and overcome obstacles?
- successfully prioritized your workload?
- adapted quickly to a change of plans?
- been involved in a change management project?
- been in a leadership position?
- had international experience?
- shown dedication and commitment to a project?
- gone beyond the call of duty?
- been passionate about your product or service?
- won awards recognizing your outstanding performance?
- obtained extra skills or certifications, or pursued hobbies?

Being able to accomplish these things does involve skill – but more importantly it speaks to attitude. **Attitude** is important in traditional industry as well, but it's so much more so in the New Economy because of the current lack of general experience. That means many companies are looking for potential.

You can't obtain a certificate proving you have potential to your prospective employer, but you can, and should, use anything in your past that supports your claim to have it. Your goal should be to answer yes to as many points on the list above as you can. And you should come up with some examples of your own. Don't be afraid to blow your own trumpet. Ask friends to help you if you're stuck. Commercial experience is always preferable, but if your current job isn't likely to put you in these situations, use examples from your daily life to prove your point. For some entry-level positions, volunteer experience is acceptable, whether in a non-profit or education setting.

Skilling up

No one can really teach you how to have potential or the right attitude. But there's plenty of literature on the shelves to help you learn some of the right habits. One thing does seem certain –

organization and practice help. If you want to become a confident leader, you should start by taking control of small projects and gaining experience that will help build your confidence. Actively seek feedback to find out where you might improve next time. Repeat as required!

If you're just out of school, pick an entry-level job that will expose you to the right environment. If you already have a job, find a way in your current job to develop these traits, even if it means volunteering some of your time. Take responsibility every chance you get. Accept leadership roles, learn to delegate effectively and inspire others. Research your industry, form opinions on where it's going. Develop your own ideas on what makes a company successful. Learn to communicate more effectively and clearly. Learn to take risks by facing up to the worst-case scenario. Target people who will appreciate your efforts and encourage you. Set goals for yourself over a specific time period.

There are many simple ways to take control of your life, but they require determination and discipline. A balanced life requires that you monitor yourself frequently, making sure all parts of your overall health and happiness are getting the attention they need. Set aside time for reflection and relaxation, to savour your achievements and plan your next challenge. Be prepared to change your own priorities if something isn't working for you – and remember to differentiate between short-term and long-term goals. Sometimes short-term sacrifices are necessary to achieve a greater good. Set benchmarks and timetables to mark progress and remember to reward yourself along the way, a powerful incentive to carry on when you feel like giving up. Appendix 1 has some more on specific books you can try.

part three
opportunities

chapter seven
what suits you?

New job opportunities for:

- Business analysts
- Journalists
- Magazine editors
- TV producers
- Party hosts
- Graphic designers
- Public relations agents
- Account executives
- Media buyers
- Business development
- Marketing managers
- Brand managers
- Lawyers
- Sales reps
- Librarians

The next few chapters will go into detail on each of these fronts but here's a quick sampling of the type of jobs that can be easily converted from Old Economy positions to New Economy ones:

- **Business analyst** to **Dot com business development analyst:** Track trends and spot business opportunities in cyberspace.

- **Journalist** to **Website content writer:** Report on internet e-commerce issues or other topics. Repurpose content from other sources.

- **Magazine editor** to **Content supervisor:** Oversee content development, manage staff, acquire new material, forge alliances.

- **TV producer** to **Channel producer, website producer:** Oversee technical and content teams at a large dot com or with a web agency.

- **Party host** to **Web chat host:** Monitor chat rooms for appropriate behaviour, ask questions to stimulate discussion.

- **Graphic designer** to **Web designer, multimedia designer:** Use software programs to design banner ads, websites and graphics, and create animations.

- **Public relations agent** to **Dot com PR agent:** Represent New Media companies including dot coms and IT-related businesses.

- **Account executive** to **New Media agency account executive:** Handle clients who want to advertise on the web.

- **Media buyer/planner** to **New Media buyer:** Plan campaigns on the web, negotiate with portals for banner advertising placement.

- **Business development manager** to **E-commerce, t-commerce or m-commerce business development manager:** Come up with a New Economy revenue strategy for a dot com or traditional company looking to break into the internet or other technology such as wireless or interactive television.

- **Marketing manager** to **E-marketing manager:** Come up with a strategy to market your company's products on the internet.

- **Brand manager** to **Dot com brand manager:** Establish and build a brand for a dot com.

- **Lawyer** to **New Media lawyer:** Specialize in privacy, e-commerce and cyberspace issues, represent software and hardware companies.

- **Sales rep** to **Dot com sales rep:** Explain highly technical products in terms people can understand and that will make them want to buy.

- **Librarian** to **Web directory planner:** Work for a listing service such as Yahoo! to categorize the vast amounts of information on the web.

chapter eight
jobs in depth

marketing, sales, business development, content, public relations

◆ Marketing

◆ Sales

◆ Business development

◆ Content

◆ Public relations

Marketing

Some of the most common New Economy jobs started off as traditional industry jobs, then morphed to include new technology and its applications. Because of that, employees with core skills in areas such as marketing are finding it easy to apply those skills to internet-based environments. In this section we'll look at some commonly advertised marketing positions – the roles and responsibilities.

Marketing has always been key to a company's success, but with dot coms it's crucial. Unlike the off-line world where market leaders already exist, and marketing patterns and practices are well established, the rules in the online world have yet to be written. The early thinking was that old marketing rules should be thrown out altogether, but more recently people are saying that some old-style brand-building techniques may be effective after all.

NEW ECONOMY SNAPSHOT

An August 2000 report by the Internet Advertising Bureau showed the value of online advertising rising rapidly. First-quarter online advertising revenues for 2000 amounted to $1.953 billion, almost $1 billion more than the same period in 1999. Advertising revenues from the fourth quarter of 1999 showed a rise of 9.9 per cent, while the first quarter of 1999 revealed a comparative rise of 182 per cent. The report shows that online advertisers are resorting to more creative methods in trying to get their message across to customers. The study tracked referral ads, keyword searches, and classifieds – as well as traditional banner ads, sponsorships and e-mail. The banner ad is still the number one tool for online advertisers.

Because of that, people with classic marketing training and experience (especially in fast-moving consumer goods, which are well suited to online sales) can use their experience to great effect.

Direct Recruitment, an agency specializing in marketing staff, says on its website (*www.direct-recruitment.co.uk*): 'Currently there is a distinct dearth of people on the market to meet the demands of the advances in new technology and the significant growth in data-driven marketing. More companies and industry sectors than ever before are relying on relationship marketing techniques to build brand awareness, to maintain their position in the marketplace, to reduce expenditure and to increase bottom line profitability. Many more of our clients – both agencies and client companies – are realizing that their most valuable resource, their data, needs to be understood, managed and utilized properly, and are willing to pay good salaries for people who can do so.' (More on this in Chapter 17.)

There are a range of companies to choose from: well-established dot com brands such as Amazon, traditional retailers such as Sainsbury's selling groceries online, major brands such as Procter and Gamble looking to develop an online presence, or small start-ups where the entire marketing and maybe sales staff consists of you! Your first step is to decide which kind of company would suit you best, and how much responsibility you want.

NEW ECONOMY SNAPSHOT

The e-mail marketing industry will be worth $4.5 billion by 2003, according to an October 2000 report released by eMarketer. Spending on e-mail advertising alone is expected to reach $2 billion by 2003. eMarketer predicts that e-mail advertising will account for a larger share of web advertising in the future. Revenue from e-mail advertising is expected to rise from five per cent of total web advertising in 1999 to 13 per cent in 2003.

As previously mentioned, during the first few years of the e-commerce explosion, a flood of business-to-consumer websites rushed to market. The shakedown during 2000 was swift and brutal, with thousands of jobs lost as a result. The surviving companies emerged more stable; however, in the aftermath, many analysts began to favour business-to-business retailers, among other areas (see Chapter 13). Make sure you screen your potential employers carefully.

Typical marketing manager jobs require classical skills – managing budgets, partner relationships, agency relationships, sales strategies and customer relationships – adapted to an online setting. Employees must be able to cope with the collapsed time frame of decision-making and the fact that the environment often has no precedent or formal procedures. Attitude and enthusiasm are important, as is the ability to be a team player. Pan-European experience and client-side skills are at a premium. Here are some typical examples of marketing jobs from pricejamieson's website (*www.pricejam.com*):

Marketing Manager – Salary £40,000

One of the UK's leading online newspapers is seeking a Marketing Manager to develop and execute strategic marketing plans for their network, setting targets. You will manage the budget, and strategic partner relationships, including affiliate marketing partners, and multiple service providers, including advertising, PR and online agencies. The role is multifaceted and also will include the development and implementation of acquisition and retention strategies, advertising, relationship marketing, promotions, corporate identity, trade marketing, publicity and events. You will be a champion of the consumer, ensuring the business is consumer focused. You will have a strong understanding of and experience with launching and building brands and customer relationship management, and be able to grasp the 'big picture' and develop strategies for achieving the longer-term vision for the business. This is a fantastic opportunity for a formally trained marketer to grow with the business and achieve a director-level position within 12–18 months.

Marketing executives are in high demand and although the salary scales are lower, so are the number of years' experience required. Salaries range from £20–25,000. At the other end, classically trained **marketing directors** can command as high as £70,000 plus stock options.

Sales & Marketing Manager – Salary £35,000

A Sales and Marketing Manager is needed for a global application service provider with a range of proprietary software targeted at large financial institutions. Main tasks will involve: organization of market research for all products, execution of all marketing campaigns and working with the Market and Sales Director for winning and retaining major institutional clients. You must have previous city-based financial marketing experience.

At a time when many websites are having trouble surviving, online advertising is proving profitable for direct marketers, according to an August 2000 survey by the Direct Marketing Association which found that 70 per cent of **direct marketers** made online profits in 2000, up from just 49 per cent the year before. The most recommended ways of driving sales were through search engine positioning and direct e-mail to customers and site visitors. While the latter was used more frequently, the former was found to be more effective. Catalogues remain the most important way of driving traffic to a website. As for the future, 86 per cent of direct marketers said interactive media has the most potential to generate revenue over the next three years.

Direct Campaign Manager, Personal Market – Salary £35,000

Market-leading innovative mobile company requires individual with 4-5 years' marketing experience (and at least two within a direct marketing environment) to manage direct marketing campaigns and below-the-line activities for products, propositions and services relating to the personal market segments.

Establishing **brand** is the holy grail for most start-ups. No longer able to rely on an underdeveloped market and little competition, many are struggling to make themselves known and are using traditional marketing techniques to help get there.

Brand Manager – Salary £60,000

Our client offers a range of market-leading internet and mobile internet services. The purpose of this role is to ensure that the brand strategy is successfully communicated throughout Europe … working with market research departments [to] ensure fast, measurable feedback of campaigns' successes and brand perception is delivered; help ensure that the development and integrity of the brand fulfils company objectives; monitor budgets to ensure that cost-effective and timely activity is achieved in each country. The ideal candidate will be a graduate, have a minimum 3–5 years in a consumer-brand-orientated marketing department or agency; be experienced manager of significant international budgets through a wide range of above-the-line media; have proven experience of being able to successfully contribute to brand strategy and development in a dynamic environment; and be multilingual.

Sales

Good sales people have always been important in traditional business and it's no less so for New Economy companies, especially as the markets get more competitive. Being a good communicator and confident presenter is valuable. Being able to explain technically complicated material in a clear, understandable fashion is critical if you are going to represent New Economy companies. Negotiation skills are an asset as are relationship-building and team-playing skills. Being able to juggle many tasks at once is also important. Salaries range from £18–£20,000 at the **executive** level to £35–45,000 at the **manager** level.

One New Media recruitment firm put it right in their ad:

'New Media jobs have been getting a lot of press in the last couple of months. We are currently recruiting for a large number of the big names in the New Media marketplace, as well as some of the lesser-known, up-and-coming internet companies. Not all New Media jobs require previous online experience although a sound understanding of the internet and the commercial opportunities it represents is essential.'

The New Media Partnership deals with online sales vacancies. Here's a selection of jobs from the websites of The New Media Partnership (*www.the-media-partnership.com*) and pricejamieson (*www.pricejam.com*) to give you an idea of what the roles are and what kind of experience is typically necessary:

Account Handler – Salary £25,000 + £10,000 commission

Two years or more good media sales experience. Online experience isn't necessary but a good understanding of the issues involved is. This role is working for one of the large internet sales houses and as such requires a board-level presenter who will be able to represent the company at a high level. Representing a portfolio of sites, a large number of which will be household names, the successful candidate will be given online training and the opportunity to become an experienced professional in the New Media field. The successful candidate is likely to be DIPADA or AIDA trained, hardworking and very bright and enthusiastic.

Online Client Sales Manager – Salary to £40,000 basic + car allowance, bonus, benefits and phantom equity scheme

Working for one of the biggest names in media, you will be an experienced manager and will have at least four or five years' media experience. Previous online experience is not a pre-requisite but an understanding of the online issues is. Able to think strategically across other revenue streams and keen to get involved in emerging platforms.

Account Manager – £25–30,000 + benefits

Excellent relationship-building skills. Responsible for co-ordinating and developing accounts. The key thing is to ensure successful delivery of all projects and grow opportunities for future business. Work closely with design teams on conceptual work and brainstorming, involved in strategic direction of new concepts. Need excellent team-working and communications skills and be able to deal with many tasks.

Business development

This area is worth mentioning separately from marketing and sales because while it draws on those skills, it has emerged as its own discipline in the New Economy. In the face of constant industry change and innovation, companies need to have staff who can track development in-house around the clock. Business development directors, consultants, managers and executives are needed all across the board. A typical ad:

Business Development Manager – Salary to £35,000 + commission + benefits

Working alongside the Business Development Director you will be looking at alternative sources of revenue for a small portfolio of successful websites. Evaluating existing partnerships and pitching for new ones will be just one of your areas of responsibility. Natural sales skills and creative thinking are pre-requisites for this challenging role.

At a **director** level, which can pay up to £60,000, the job consists of growing company business, defining product offerings, forming strategic alliances, negotiating and closing deals. Typically you need excellent team skills, initiative, excellent presentation and negotiating skills and a high degree of business and industry awareness.

At a **manager** level, where salaries are typically around £35,000, you will typically manage relationships with strategic partners and clients, chart new opportunities, pinpoint new clients and manage contract negotiations.

As an **analyst** you can make up to £30,000 supporting business development by analyzing commercial opportunities, and researching deal structuring and negotiation.

At an **executive level** you can make about £25,000 identifying new markets and opportunities for your company. At this level determination and a strong desire to succeed can make up for a lack of experience.

Content

It's a cliché to say that content is king, but it's true. Someone's got to produce the information for the Information Superhighway. There are lots of opportunities for people with experience in producing content for traditional media outlets, or wanting to get in at an entry-level position.

There has been an explosion in demand for information about e commerce and the internet, as businesses attempt to find winning business strategies.

Financial information services have proliferated. Companies with strong off-line brands have also taken to the web to find new ways of interacting with their customers – for example women's and teen websites. Industries have flocked to cyberspace – gardening, building, across every retail sector. Journalists with experience in a particular beat can find work without having direct experience in online writing. Some basic HTML and layout experience is an asset, as is the ability to prioritize in an environment where the deadlines are immediate.

Web editor jobs may include responsibility for technical teams as well as content since the two can be inseparable online. In this case, a thorough knowledge of what the technologies are capable of is an asset. Some knowledge of design is also beneficial.

As a beat writer or **copy-editor** your salary is typically £25–£30,000 with **editor** salaries starting at £30–£35,000.

The more senior the job, the more strategic skills are required in terms of marrying content, technology and potential audience. For example as a senior editor of a music website you might consider whether you can present your content in a compelling way over a mobile phone or limit your offering to a PC-based environment.

Managing Editor – Salary £50,000

If you have a degree plus at least two years' experience as a Managing Editor in a publishing house and a keen interest in technical developments and strong organizational skills, we would like very much to hear from you. Working closely with other members of the division and the key publishing functions within our company, you will spearhead our entrance into the new and exciting world of e-books. You will co-ordinate publishing plans, be involved in the procurement of appropriate rights and negotiating royalties, oversee the digitization of texts and assist in arrangements for the sale of e-books through both existing and new channels. You will also be prominent in the development of our ongoing e-book strategy.

For people involved in television production, the move to the web is a natural one as it requires many of the same project management skills that television shows do: managing teams, setting goals, meeting targets, setting budgets, overseeing technical teams, determining editorial direction. In addition to these jobs there has been an explosion in the number of people needed to acquire and manage non-original content, since many websites choose to buy syndicated or independently produced copy rather than generate it in-house.

Producer – Salary £30–35,000 + health, pension

An Editorial Producer for one of the top three women's retail portals, you will have day-to-day responsibility for the editorial content, production and management for three channels. Working closely with the Editorial Director and Business Development team, you will secure content partners that reflect the target audience. Objects are to maintain high levels of site users and participants in commercial opportunities to be found on this lifestyle portal.

Content Manager – Salary £35,000

This wireless internet start-up wants a Content Manager who will be responsible for making alliances with companies that provide product-based information (data) and other content. This individual must have good interpersonal and commercial/negotiation skills. You will also have experience in managing a small team of people and working with external clients. Must have a degree.

Public relations

As with editorial, public relations employees can apply their traditional skills to New Media clients.

PR account managers and executives for New Economy firms have the additional challenge of working to intense deadlines in a fluctuating environment. Being able to network and form a solid contact list is essential.

Salaries for **executives** range from £16,000 to £20,000, rising to £30,000 to £35,000 for **managers**. For **directors**, salaries can go as high as £50,000.

For more senior levels you may be required to have pan-European experience as well as experience of outsourcing PR functions to agencies. Knowing how to create a buzz in both the industry and consumer press will catapult you up the ladder in today's highly competitive environment.

Account Manager – Salary £26,000

Experienced campaign manager required for this excellent consultancy's technology and telecoms team. Working on a mix of technology and New Media clients, you will need solid b2b and b2c skills as well as strategic flair and a down-to-earth attitude.

'Experience is not such a vital component in the recruitment methodology of Jobsite as there are very few people with vast amounts of experience within the internet and even online recruitment, so I would say that vision and understanding of the business are equally as important as experience ... The people we look for are people who constantly look for opportunities and can demonstrate team spirit. They tend to be hungry for success in a challenging environment.'

Zoe Barnes, GoJobsite

opportunities

fromheretoe

momentum

jobs in depth

web jobs

- Web designer

- Web developer/programmer

- Site manager/webmaster

- Other IT positions

NEW ECONOMY SNAPSHOT

USA-based business Network Solutions registers a new dot com company every 3.9 seconds.

As the number of websites in cyberspace grows, so does the need for people to build and maintain them. Not so long ago entire sites were handled by a webmaster alone, responsible for all content as well as layout. Those situations still exist but the vast majority of commercial sites are increasingly sophisticated, requiring ever-larger teams with specialized skills to build the sites and keep them running smoothly. Whether a company hires staff in-house or outsources the technical work, the job pool just keeps growing.

The computer and data processing sector in the USA will have the highest growth rate of any industry from now until 2008, according to the US Department of Labor's 1999 study. Predicted growth for the sector is 117 per cent and demand for skilled high-tech employees will grow accordingly. The numbers of computer engineers will increase by 108 per cent, while growth of 102 per cent is expected in the numbers of support specialists. There will be 94 per cent more systems analysts in 2008, 77 per cent more database administrators and 73 per cent more desktop publishing specialists.

Large firms will fuel the growth in IT jobs over the next four years, according to a recent report by Cahners In-Stat Group. IT spending among companies with over 1000 employees is set to increase by eight per cent a year until 2004. Mid-sized firms (100–999 employees) will increase annual spending on IT jobs by three per cent, while small companies (5–99 employees) will spend one per cent more each year. The report says larger firms will spend more because they are less likely to outsource IT operations and tend to invest heavily in internal infrastructures. However, big companies are expected to outsource non-strategic functions such as help-desk support and remote office administration. In the future, the IT workforce of large companies will consist mainly of senior and highly skilled personnel. IT employment will not increase significantly among mid-sized companies, with pay rises accounting for the three per cent annual spending rise. As the IT skills shortage increases, many of these companies will outsource data centre and e-commerce services.

Beyond the web, there's also a growing need for people to build and maintain the computer systems that make the internet possible. Building the backbone requires a lot of high-tech help. Companies are become increasingly networked, within their own environment

opportunities

from here to

momentum

Demand for skilled IT workers in the USA this year is set to far exceed supply, leaving 843,000 of 1.6 million new IT jobs unfilled, according to a July 2000 report from the Information Technology Association of America. The shortfall means that one in every 12 IT jobs will have been vacant during 2000. Seventy per cent of new IT jobs will be with smaller non-IT firms looking for technical support and system administration help. Thirteen per cent of the new IT vacancies are for workers with web-related skills. Database development and software engineering jobs account for a further 20 per cent of the IT vacancies.

and with their strategic partners. However, there's a reason there's a skill shortage, and that's because skill is required. If you want to make a move into these areas you will have to get formal professional training in your particular area of interest for anything beyond entry-level jobs.

Here are some of the IT positions, starting with the ones that are web-based, and most easily broken into.

Web designer

Web designers come up with the look and feel of the website. Their primary purpose is to make the site attractive and workable. It's relatively easy for people with training in graphic design to bring those skills to web work, but it requires knowledge of the new tools. Computer skills required include HTML and HTML editors such as FrontPage, animation programs such as Flash and Fireworks, graphic design programs such as Adobe Photoshop, Illustrator and Freehand, and website design programs such as Macromedia's Dreamweaver. Designers need to be familiar with both Mac and PC platforms. Some experience with the layout program QuarkXPress would be advantageous. Programming and scripting languages such as Perl, JavaScript and Java are in hot demand – not expected, but a bonus.

Multimedia designers should have an understanding of 3D animation and video and might be expected to know video management programs such as Adobe Premiere, Quick Time and G2 (Real Audio and Video) and Macromedia Director. An understanding of digital video editing systems such as Avid and effects programs such as AfterEffects is needed for video-based work.

For entry-level jobs you won't be expected to have a portfolio of commercial experience but for anything mid-level you will. Having a degree in graphic design and a portfolio will get you interviews.

Designers are expected to show creativity, be self-motivated, and be able to work as part of a team and be articulate. Higher-up positions might require client-facing skills.

Managers surveyed by the Information Technology Association of America say the skills they seek in new IT hires are, in order: a good knowledge base in the relevant area, hands-on experience, good communication, problem-solving and analytical skills, along with flexibility, and the ability to learn quickly.

Web Designer – Salary £35,000

A top designer is needed to take existing print to new levels on different platforms (WAP/web/interactive) and on a new product … [The candidate will have] three years' HTML hand-coded experience [using] HTML 3 and 4, scripting languages, three years' commercial web experience, proven web design capabilities (creative and commercial), Photoshop, Illustrator, Flash, Dreamweaver, CorelDraw, animation skills, 3D skills. [Also needed:] proven technical skills (custom languages), project management skills (product life cycle), must have worked on at least two different platforms, good organization skills/team player, with ability to work with programmers to see projects through from implementation to completion. Creative/inventive/original.

Web developer/programmer

Web developers and programmers are in hottest demand as a rule, and with the right level of experience they can often write their own tickets. These people write and maintain the computer programs that underpin a website. They are responsible for conceiving and developing the interface it presents to the public and maximizing its efficiency.

Solid computer skills are essential. Candidates need the basic web-based programs including HTML, Flash, Photoshop, Illustrator, Dreamweaver, Fireworks, Shockwave, Flash, Director, HTML and HTTP.

They also need to know scripting and programming languages such as JavaScript, CGI scripts and ASP as well as Perl and Java. Familiarity with traditional programming languages such as C and C++ are an added bonus.

Developers should also be familiar with business applications and database systems. The latter can lead to a position as a database administrator, a person who manages and interprets the information about a website's users – an increasingly critical tool used by companies looking to improve on performance.

Organizational skills and an attention to detail are also of paramount importance, as is the ability to work without supervision as well as part of a team under intense deadline pressure. Typically developers who want to move up the ladder must show management skills, often by becoming team leaders on the life cycle of specific projects. Communication skills are important as team leaders typically have to interact with people such as clients or content developers who may be unfamiliar with technical details.

Salaries start at about £26,000, moving up to £35,000 at an intermediate level and £45,000 and beyond for senior developers. Here's a typical ad from pricejamieson's boards:

Technical Developer – Salary £30,000

The role will be very hands-on and requires the candidate to evaluate all the current backend systems and re-work/improve them. We are also looking for someone who can implement his or her own ideas in what is a technically creative role. Commercial experience required. The candidate will have one year's experience of MySQL, ASP, HTML, Java, Perl, PHP3/4, XML (not a must), ASP, DHTML, JavaScript, and the UNIX and NT 4.0 environments.

Site manager/webmaster

Site managers oversee the whole production from a technical and editorial point of view. The job is a more sophisticated version of what webmasters used to do single-handedly. Often coming from the designer or developer ranks, having worked as team leaders, site managers combine a thorough technical background with classic management skills and an understanding of content. Typically the site manager is responsible for strategic development – picking the platforms and protocols that the site will use – as well as overseeing its day-to-day maintenance. They will be up on the latest standards all across the board, from protocols on data exchange to knowing what various server platforms have to offer. Candidates should also know how to manage a team and a project. Communication and presentation skills are very important – in the senior technical positions candidates need to know how to communicate complicated technical issues to non-technical people such as clients. Some knowledge of e-commerce concepts and business practices is also essential at this level. Salaries can range from £45,000.

Site Manager – Salary £45,000

This company [is] currently looking for a technical manager/director to take over the technical management and strategic development of our ten websites. We require a dynamic, enthusiastic individual who has at least two years' experience working as the technical lead on a busy website. Detailed knowledge and experience of HTML, UNIX, SQL and dynamic web publishing is essential. The successful candidate will probably be well versed in Perl and/or C and have experience of programming CGIs and other server-side applications. A knowledge of Java, JavaScript and PHP3 querying of SQL would also be an advantage.

Other IT positions

In addition to jobs centred on the maintenance of websites, there are classic computer jobs available in abundance as more companies begin to get wired and use increasingly sophisticated programs. These are the classic IT jobs, with positions ranging from basic system administration – making sure all the computer systems work together with each other – to those specializing in areas such as networking – the development of Local Area Networks within companies which let employees share computer files on common hard drives.

NEW ECONOMY SNAPSHOT

IDC predicts the internetworking area will experience the most acute skills shortage by the year 2002. Demand for IT skills in Western Europe is expected to grow from approximately 9.47 million IT professionals in 1999 to 13.07 million in 2003 while supply is set to grow from 8.61 million to 11.33 million in 2003. 1.7 million jobs will be unfilled. In the UK, as demand hits 2,348,827 in 2003, there will be a shortage of 329,573 people, or 14 per cent of the desired workforce.

part four
acquiring new skills

chapter ten
becoming computer-friendly

- ◆ Before you buy

- ◆ Peripherals

- ◆ Getting connected

- ◆ Surfing the web

- ◆ Building a website

Learning to use a computer and negotiate your way around the internet is obviously critical to anyone entering the dot com world. The level of familiarity required will depend on the job you are applying for, but a thorough knowledge of technology and computing is important for all jobs, even if you don't plan on writing code. Anyone involved in e-commerce or with a dot com has to be aware of the technical capabilities of the equipment – it's no good having a brilliant idea if it can't be executed, as some high-profile multi-million pound failures have proven. In addition, you can't always rely on a separate technical staff to deal with every issue – often there just isn't the time or manpower to have someone install the program or configure the network for you. The more you know, the more power you have in your own hands. First off, buy a computer, if you haven't already.

Before you buy

Decide what you need. If you are planning to work from home, don't scrimp – this will be your main business investment in yourself. Inferior equipment will just slow you down. If you don't have the money, consider getting a loan to make purchases possible. (You'll need all the latest software as well.) Depending on your tax status you may be able to deduct some of the cost from your income. Consult an accountant. If you have one main employer, consider asking them to help you pay part of the costs for equipment specific to their projects.

When picking a product do read the fine print. Ask around for product recommendations and read up in the plethora of magazines currently available. Read the newsgroups and find out what users have to say. Trade fairs are a great place to get deals on components once you know what you are looking for. Keep an eye in the papers for announcements. There are dozens of local websites with product reviews and deals. ZDNet has a UK-based site (*www.zdnet.co.uk*) with lots of information. Also worth considering:

- ◆ *ukpc.net*
- ◆ *www.ukcomputers.co.uk*
- ◆ *www.bestpricecomputers.ltd.uk*
- ◆ *uk.shopsmart.com*
- ◆ *www.buy-com.co.uk*
- ◆ *ukmobiles.com.*

When you shop, come armed with a list of questions and be firm with sales people who confuse you with jargon or who are evasive. Never buy a product without getting all the information you need – it can be a very expensive mistake. By asking in advance when advice is free you can avoid paying for expensive help-line service after the fact, a common pitfall among computer purchasers. Try to get all your hardware and software questions dealt with before the warrantee or free help period expires.

acquiring new skills

from here to e

momentum

Here are some basic questions to resolve before you buy:

◆ **Laptop or desktop:** Laptops are convenient and space-efficient but peripherals such as modems, CD-ROM players, printers and the like are cheaper if you buy a desktop model, as is the computer itself.

◆ **Mac or PC:** Many people prefer Macs for graphic designs, but IBM computers and their peripherals are usually cheaper, given that many companies manufacture IBM-compatible equipment. If you are planning to do artwork, it's worth considering the advantages a Mac has to offer.

◆ **Package deals:** With PCs, you can choose between buying a computer with all the components thrown in or buying the bits separately. The advantage of a package is that it is usually cheaper, but the components may not be name brand. However, they may still be perfectly acceptable for your needs. Do your research on each component – especially what kind of monitor, sound card, modem and CD-ROM player it comes equipped with, and decide if it's worth the price-quality compromise.

◆ **Memory:** Buy as much as you can afford. Basic RAM (Random Access Memory, used by the computer to temporarily store data or programs) should be no less than 32 megabytes and a decent hard drive should hold at least 2 gigabytes of information.

Peripherals

Modems

A critical purchase, if you are planning to use your telephone line to get connected. They come in speeds of up to 56Kbps. Get the fastest you can afford. There are other connection technologies for high-speed service but not all are widely available yet. Cable modems show promise and companies are in the process of rolling out the technology. Satellite companies are looking into systems that will let you access the internet through a set-top box. Watch for developments.

Sound cards/video cards

They come in a variety of shapes and sizes, depending on how advanced you need your system to be. If you are hoping to watch

movies or do advanced editing on your system you can get excellent
equipment at top dollar rates. If you're just planning to listen to
online radio stations or MP3 files, you may choose to settle for
something middle or lower-end.

CD-ROM drives

Some computers come with CD-ROM drives that can write on to
rewritable or one-time only disks as well as read them. You can make
your own CDs for fun or for self-promotion. Many companies
distribute CDs promoting their company – why not make one
containing your résumé and samples of your work? Rewritable CDs
can be an excellent way of storing large files, especially music or
photograph files, which won't fit on a floppy.

Zip drives

Another storage solution. These drives basically extend your hard
drive.

Printers

Laser printers offer better resolution than the bubble-jet variety but
the low-end models are typically only black and white. For colour,
bubble-jets tend to be more affordable.

Scanners

Another fun toy and business tool, enabling you to scan documents
or pictures into digital files you can e-mail to friends or co-workers.

Getting connected

To get on to the internet you need an internet service provider (ISP)
that acts as your gateway to the network. There is an array of options
to choose from. Key factors to consider include basic price and the
availability of customer service. Depending on the amount you use
the internet you should consider whether you want to be billed for
specific hours or buy a fixed amount per month. If you are accessing
the internet via a regular phone line you may also be charged the
regular cost of a local phone call, although there are moves afoot to

offer unmetered access. There are packages available that will discount the cost of your calls at certain rates depending on the time of day. Check what cable and satellite companies have to offer. For more information on ISPs, search the web and consult trade magazines and internet guidebooks (see Appendix 1).

Surfing the web

To surf the web once you're connected you need a **browser**, which usually comes preinstalled in most computers. If it hasn't, your main choices are Netscape Navigator and Internet Explorer, both downloadable for free (*www.netscape.com* and *www.microsoft.com*). Both come with a variety of optional programs such as instant messaging. Since both programs have their strengths and weaknesses it's worth installing them both, especially if you are doing your own website and want to see how it looks on both systems.

Beyond basic surfing you'll need a few other programs to make your experience a **multimedia** one. Start with these:

◆ RealPlayer for streaming audio and video (*www.real.com*)

◆ Shockwave Flash and Director (*www.macromedia.com*) for nifty animation

◆ Quicktime (*www.apple.com/quicktime/*) for viewing movies

◆ Winamp (*www.winamp.com*) or other MP3 music player for playing audio files.

Other useful programs include:

◆ Adobe Acrobat reader (*www.adobe.com*) for viewing documents in this format (called pdf); often used by government sites

◆ Adobe Photoshop (*www.adobe.com*) graphics program for altering photographs and making GIF and JPEG graphics

◆ an FTP program such as WS-FTP (*www.wsftp.com*) to download and upload files from servers

◆ WinZip (*www.winzip.com*) or other compression software which lets you unzip/zip compressed files

◆ Napster (*www.napster.com*) music-swapping program – for fun, and a sense of what so-called peer-to-peer networking is all about.

Building a website

Anyone wanting to plunge into the world of the web should build their own website. For non-core IT, non-web design jobs it doesn't have to be very sophisticated and there are many places to start. Some ISPs have their own programs that let you build a site through a template, letting those without HTML skills build basic pages. I would recommend learning basic HTML as well as using web-building software. Information, tutorials and manuals are widely available on the web. Webmonkey (*www.webmonkey.com*) is a good place to start (see Appendix 1 for more).

A WORD ABOUT HTML

Hypertext Mark-Up Language is very straightforward. See it for yourself. In the toolbar of your browser select Source or Page Source in the View menu. You'll see a rundown of all the code required to generate the page you're looking at. How it works is simple:

The code that makes the web page display information is contained within a 'tag' like this: <command>

followed by a counter-command like this: </command>.

For example if you wanted to make text bold you would do this: <b> text here! </b> ('b' is the code for BOLD)

When you write an HTML document you can do it with the help of any number of sophisticated authoring programs, or you can simply write it in

Notepad, save it as an .htm or .html file and view it through your browser.

The overall structure to an HTML document starts with <HTML> and ends with </HTML>. Everything in between is a variation on that theme!

Both Netscape and Internet Explorer come with HTML editors that make the work simpler. For more go to:

◆ Microsoft Frontpage (*www.microsoft.com*)
◆ Netscape Communicator (*www.netscape.com*).

More sophisticated software used by the industry (with free downloadable trial versions) includes:

◆ Macromedia's Dreamweaver (*www.macromedia.com*)
◆ Allaire's HomeSite (*www.allaire.com*)
◆ Adobe's GoLive (*www.adobe.com*).

Do a photo album, write a treatise, collect your favourite links – it doesn't really matter what your content is as long as you try all the tools and get a feel for what website construction is all about.

If you're hoping to make a career out of doing websites, try getting started by volunteering to build one for a non-profit group. Some entry-level jobs will accept non-commercial experience. Your goal should be to become familiar with as many of the authoring tools and options as possible. Formal courses can accelerate learning tremendously – but choose carefully to make sure it's absolutely relevant to what you need to know. More on educational qualifications in Chapter 12.

chapter eleven
becoming technology-literate

- ◆ Wireless

- ◆ Interactive digital television

- ◆ Broadband

- ◆ Computer hardware/software issues

- ◆ Internet infrastructure

- ◆ Privacy, security and consumer issues

Keeping up to date on developments in the New Economy – whether it's following e-commerce trends or the latest technological developments – is a full-time affair. Needless to say, it's essential to keep current. You don't need to know every technical twitch unless you want to be a hard-core expert. But you do need as in-depth an understanding as you can find the time for to know what's technically feasible at the moment and in the future. You should read New Economy magazines such as *Business 2.0*, *Industry Standard*, *New Media Age* and *Revolution*, to name just a few of the leading titles. Subscribe to a technology newsletter such as CNET's *digital dispatch* (*www.cnet.com*) or one of ZDNet's (*www.zdnet.com*). And keep an eye out for the latest New Economy titles from ft.com (which shares a publisher with this book!). See Appendix 1 for additional reading suggestions.

Any notes on what's hot and what's not on a high-tech front will be immediately dated, so it's imperative you learn the trends yourself.

That said, here are some areas to watch as of this writing. (Also see Chapter 13.)

Wireless

Many firms are putting their money – and lots of it – into mobile technologies. The phenomenal success of **NTT DoCoMo's i-Mode** mobile telephone platform in Japan has Europe scrambling to find the same success. The platform used in Europe is known as WAP (**Wireless Application Protocol**) and is having teething pains but development continues. With the high penetration of mobile phones in Europe as opposed to North America, many see the market as one of the most developed worldwide. What kind of content wireless applications can and should deliver is *the* big question.

Do customers want to use their phones to surf the web and read e-mail? Play games? Perhaps the most important question from an e-commerce point of view is, will customers shop on their phones? Are mobile communications applications or information applications? How can you type a letter into those tiny keypads? Mobile **pagers** such as RIM's Blackberry come with bigger keypads – will they rival the mobile phone? And what about the growing popularity of the **Personal Digital Assistant** (PDA) such as PalmPilots or Britain's own Psion?

NEW ECONOMY SNAPSHOT

Sixty-two per cent of UK companies have shelved plans for mobile commerce for the moment, according to an October survey of 500 UK companies conducted for e-business Expo 2000, *Computer Weekly* and Compaq. Twenty per cent of the companies said the technology had yet to prove itself; 19 per cent said they didn't have the budget, while 18 per cent said they didn't have the staff; 17 per cent said upper management remained unconvinced; 31 per cent were concentrating on other areas. However 22 per cent expected to use WAP in the future; 11 per cent planned to make use of Bluetooth and 3G, and nine per cent will use GPRS 9. Forty-four per cent thought m-commerce would bring better customer service; 37 per cent said it would give them a competitive advantage; 30 per cent said it would help them access new markets.

Interactive digital television

Television is being transformed by digital as well and the race to develop so-called t-commerce options is well underway. With the

British government committed to switching off the analogue signal entirely in the next decade there's been renewed interest in the e-commerce potential of digital, interactive television. The medium appears to favour impulse-buying ('Watch the music video!', 'Buy the CD now!'). The market is currently bogged down in technical issues, including which platform offers better service – satellite, cable or digital terrestrial. The lack of common standards is deterring some advertisers from spending money across all platforms. The expense of set-top boxes and the lack (so far) of compelling content are currently holding back growth.

Broadband

NEW ECONOMY SNAPSHOT

As of October 2000, only one per cent of UK homes had a broadband connection compared to six per cent of homes in the USA and 3.2 per cent in Germany, according to research from internet measurement firm, NetValue.

Increasing the internet's capacity to carry data is an ongoing effort, and it could finally move up to the next level when true broadband access is available to every home, enabling the delivery of high-quality video on demand, and speeding up download and surfing times dramatically. Some systems offer people a permanent connection to the internet without disrupting phone service. **Fibre optic cable** – in which data is transmitted as pulses of light – is slowly being rolled out across Europe. Regular copper phone wires are being upgraded to carry more information (**DSL** – Digital Subscriber Lines). Satellite companies are experimenting with installing transmitters in set-top boxes, enabling customers to send information over the television. Microwave transmitters are cropping up in major cities, providing yet another way to send data.

Computer hardware/software issues

The need for speed is paramount and which platforms perform best is the subject of much scrutiny. Keep abreast of the latest releases in the Mac and PC worlds as well as in your favourite software. There are hundreds of websites that feature product reviews and news, including ZDNet (*www.zdnet.com*) and CNET (*www.cnet.com*). Their free newsletters offer information on a variety of specific or general topics.

Internet infrastructure

Developing a better internet backbone is also the subject of continued work, with the consortium that oversees and sets standards for the web issuing regular updates on its progress. Its current list of activities is divided into four areas: architecture, technology and society, user interface and the web accessibility initiative. The committees study everything from language protocols to e-commerce payment programs, privacy issues, graphics, internationalization issues, and mobile access and voice browsers. Location: *www.w3.org/*.

Privacy, security and consumer issues

Since security concerns, among other things, have been holding people back from embracing e-commerce, it's good to keep an eye on the latest developments in these areas. The last two years have seen marked improvements in **encryption** (translating data into code that can be re-translated on the other end with the correct 'key') and computer/server security generally, with the development of so-called '**firewalls**' which prevent unauthorized users from seeing the contents of your entire website. **Digital signatures** are being developed that could eventually have legal status. Also watch for developments in the law concerning privacy rights, child protection rights (including software that filters out selected sites), intellectual property rights and consumer standards, all of which will change the way consumers feel about shopping or collecting information online.

acquiring new skills

from here to e

momentum

chapter twelve
more on lifelong learning

- ◆ On your own
- ◆ On the job
- ◆ In full-time further education

One of the truisms about the New Economy is that as a result of its dynamic nature its workers must be constantly retraining to adapt to the changes. That means that school does not end in your teenage years or after university. From practical skills such as operating software programs, to courses on e-business at night school, the employee who wins will be the one who comes up with a plan for lifelong learning and executes it.

On your own

Put aside time for an assessment of your skills on a regular basis, looking at both the big picture (where you want to be in five years) and the small one (your day-to-day performance). By constantly asking yourself what you could learn to be more productive, you can set yourself goals to acquire specific skills and maintain a general awareness of the industry.

Set yourself goals for reading the latest industry news. A good diet would include a daily newspaper, a daily e-mail roundup of New

Economy news, a New Economy magazine a week and a book every month. There's an overwhelming amount of information out there – deciding in advance what you do and don't need to read will keep you from being overwhelmed.

Develop a routine to encourage you to skill yourself up in your free time. For example, if you regularly use certain software packages – from MS Office to Photoshop – make sure you spend time when you are not on a project deadline exploring all their features. It may seem as if there is never enough time to read the manual or take the course, but being comprehensive in your approach will give you a competitive edge. There's almost unlimited information on the web about software. Read the FAQs, check out the newsgroups and pick up new tricks for free.

Develop your own learning network, the people you can trade information with and keep current. Attend networking events in your field and never turn down an opportunity to perform a job involving a task you haven't learned before. This is true in traditional industry but even more so in the New Economy, because of its collapsed sense of time.

On the job

To keep pace with industry trends, because of the skills shortage most companies would rather skill up existing employees than hire new staff. Almost all of the bigger New Economy companies offer training days as an incentive to keep employees happy. Make sure you compare training programmes when considering a company. Some companies offer in-house scholarships for people to pursue plans that will be of use to the company. Others offer weekend retreats to develop leadership skills. Talk to your manager about the skills you think would be helpful, but bear in mind that that person will be more receptive if those skills don't stray far from your job. At smaller companies, there may not be the flexibility to release key employees for long periods of time. In this case consider doing your training outside of working hours, such as at a night school course, and ask the company to fund it in full or in part.

Find out if you qualify for any government training programmes. Many European countries, including the UK, are funding programmes to encourage people to develop New Economy skills. Ireland, for example, has a permanent council on future skills needs. Last year alone it invested £75 million in IT courses, just one of the reasons the country's New Economy is prospering. The UK government has a number of initiatives underway – check the Department for Education and Employment website (*www.dfee.gov.uk/index.shtml*).

In full-time further education

E-commerce

If your eventual aim is to be a senior corporate player in e-commerce, you should consider obtaining an MBA, as you would in traditional industry. It's fair to say the internet favours qualities that you won't be taught in business school, such as innovation and creativity, but in a knowledge-based economy, the more information you have the better, and you may make some good contacts. The professional MBA association has a website with a vast amount of information about the variety of programmes and funding options at *www.mba.org.uk*. Some companies may help fund you if you are a valuable enough asset to them, but then be prepared to offer your loyalty in return.

Core IT

For pure computing jobs, graduates are assumed to have completed the relevant courses in computer science and have learned how to build and maintain applications and networks. Companies such as

Cisco (*www.cisco.com*), Microsoft (*www.microsoft.com*), Novell (*www.novell.com*) and Oracle (*www.oracle.com*) also offer their own vendor certification schemes, at a price. Once new recruits have been hired, many companies will put them through an induction process of acquiring specific skills. For example, Cisco has set up its own academy for new employees, which provides a two-year course on networking skills. But just as people trained in business are learning about computers, so people in IT are being advised to study economics or business. Consider taking additional courses in these areas.

General

There are literally thousands of more general courses on offer. Pick up one of the publications specializing in course listings such as Floodlight or search their website at *www.floodlight.co.uk*. The choices range from full time, to night school, to online to a mixture of both. Make sure you pick the type of course that best suits your ability to learn. Do you prefer to read information or have someone talk you though it?

Some of the job portals such as Fish4jobs or agencies such as Reed or Corps offer a wide range of courses. Be sure to do your homework and ask for detailed course information – there's no shortage of people who want to help you part with your money. Monster.co.uk has good bulletin boards for people looking for answers to specific questions where you may be able to pick up some free advice.

Other educational events include seminars and trade shows. The higher-level conferences are more expensive but offer excellent bit-sized amounts of information in particular fields. They can be a goldmine of industry information, giving you access to the leading minds in the field and providing a valuable networking opportunity.

chapter thirteen
e-commerce explained

- ◆ Personalization

- ◆ Bricks and mortar versus bricks and clicks

- ◆ Fulfilment

- ◆ What sells well?

- ◆ Which platform will rule?

One of the key engines of growth in the New Economy is e-commerce. Being able to conduct commercial transactions electronically has revolutionized business practices all across the board, changing not just what we do, but the way we do it. Before embarking on your job hunt, it is important to have a thorough understanding of what exactly e-commerce is, and what – so far – it has been able to do for companies.
Consider these facts:

- ◆ E-commerce will account for 8.6 per cent of worldwide sales of goods and services by 2004, according to recent findings by Forrester Research. With internet sales of $3.2 trillion in 2004, the USA will remain the world leader in e-commerce, followed by Western Europe, where the market will be worth $1.5 trillion.

◆ The United Kingdom is still one of Europe's largest e-commerce markets with consumers spending $750 million online during 1999, according to Jupiter Media Metrix.

The internet started off as a way to exchange information in the event of a major catastrophe and developed into an information-exchange medium primarily associated with academic institutions. Seeing the internet as a platform to make money is a relatively new idea, dating from 1995, and not everyone is convinced it will work – yet.

NEW ECONOMY SNAPSHOT

A recent FT.com survey revealed that although 94 per cent of UK businesses surveyed said the internet is here to stay, 93 per cent had no plans to establish an online presence. During the summer of 2000, 32 per cent of CEOs surveyed by services company CMG had no clear idea what they were trying to achieve online.

NEW ECONOMY SNAPSHOT

Almost half the small businesses questioned in a recent survey by US incubator Xworks did not have a website, while 45 per cent could not see the benefits of having one. The survey, which consulted 250 firms, revealed that 90 per cent had underestimated the cost of setting up a website.

Business interest in the internet was initially limited to its public relations function, as a way to advertise a company for free by putting up a basic website containing corporate information. That usage still exists, but it's given way to e-commerce as the new growth industry. E-commerce, of course, refers to business and customer transactions that would have previously happened in person, by phone or some other medium and are now conducted across the net. Industries that support this function have exploded as well. According to Media Metrix there were no e-commerce sites among the top 15 websites in 1996. Now that's all there is.

NEW ECONOMY SNAPSHOT

The number of consumers visiting online stores in the UK increased by 72 per cent between January and September 2000, according to a recent survey from MMXI Europe. There were 4.3 million unique visitors to retail sites in September 2000, an increase of almost 2 million from the beginning of the year. People spent an average of 23 minutes in online retailers' sites in September, eight minutes more than they did in January.

And in spite of some holdout scepticism about the long-term viability of the internet, there's no question it's had a big impact on the world economy, particularly in the USA where it's credited for helping to propel the latest round of growth. One third of the USA's real economic growth between 1995 and 1998 came from the e-commerce and IT industries, according to the US Department of Commerce. The report also found that IT workers earned 78 per cent more than the average US worker in 1997, averaging an income of $52,920 compared to an overall average income of $29,787. E-commerce growth outstripped previous estimates by a long shot, with online sales generating between $7 billion and $15 billion toward the close of 1998. Predictions had been that e-commerce would not generate $7 billion in sales until 2000. The report predicts that by 2006 almost half of all US workers will work in industries that either produce IT products or use IT products extensively.

In the UK the industry is just turning the corner from its heady early days, settling into a slower, steadier growth pattern. A PricewaterhouseCoopers December 2000 report found that out of 400 pure-play UK dot coms, 57 per cent are already making a profit. Dot coms selling direct products and services were having the most success with 81 per cent claiming profitability. Almost 90 per cent of the companies surveyed remain privately owned and are not planning to go public in the near future, although the majority plan to do so eventually.

While it's conventional wisdom that the internet has changed business permanently, where the profits are still remains to be seen. Here are some e-commerce trends worth thinking about.

Personalization

For the first time highly detailed data will be available about what people buy and why, and what customers want, enabling businesses to track buying patterns and viewing habits (permission-based marketing) as registration allows collection of personal information. Does the internet allow you to engage consumers in a whole new way, driving sales and marketing to a new level? Or is it just a more sophisticated way of direct mailing?

Now that consumers have a new way of spending money, how will they do it and why? Convenience? Impulse? Influenced by the vast amount of information the internet offers? How can companies and institutions help make the internet a more secure and private place, key issues to many potential online buyers?

Bricks and mortar versus bricks and clicks

Some pure-play internet companies have expanded beyond the net, forming alliances with traditional companies in retailing their goods. Strategic alliances are seen as an important way of winning market share and expanding into new markets. Over 74 per cent of New Economy companies participating in PricewaterhouseCoopers' May 2000 European Benchmarking Study formed at least one strategic alliance, many of which are international.

At the same time traditional companies are setting up e-commerce wings within their own walls. The combination of both on- and off-line retailing appears to be the wave of the future.

Fulfilment

The 1999 Christmas season was a watershed, as people trialled online shopping en masse for the first time and found the industry sorely wanting. High-profile businesses ran out of stock or didn't deliver on time, helplines were swamped or non-existent, purchasing procedures were complicated or riddled with glitches. Some companies never recovered from lost revenue; others adapted, although studies show customer service still has a long way to go, generally speaking. A recent study by BizRate.com warned that if online retailers want to maximize earnings from the predicted boom, they will need to improve the service they provide. The study revealed that an alarming 78 per cent of online shoppers abandoned shopping carts in internet stores over a 90-day period. On average, shoppers abandoned between two and three shopping carts, with each cart representing $175 in lost sales. Of those surveyed, 40 per cent said they abandoned the purchasing process because of expensive shipping and handling charges, while 21 per cent blamed slow-loading pages. How to improve feedback and ensure fulfilment remains one of the most pressing issues facing e-tailers, who are exploring everything from purchasing their own distribution networks to forming alliances with those that are already established.

NEW ECONOMY SNAPSHOT

A November 2000 e-tailing report by Ovum Research found that customer service is still poorly handled by a large number of UK e-tailing websites. Out of 114 sites surveyed all fell short in the service category. Slow response to e-mail queries, no contact phone number and poor follow-ups were amongst the most egregious mistakes made. The report warns that this will damage both the brand reputation and retail experience for e-shoppers.

What sells well?

Many existing e-commerce businesses simply replicate off-line businesses, and will only be profitable if they are able to use the net to do things faster, cheaper or more easily than what's on offer in the high street and convince customers it's worth switching over. For example, successful book and music e-tailer Amazon.com made its initial profits by shipping products directly from suppliers, bypassing the costly step of warehousing goods. It passed on the savings and convenience to customers.

Auction sites have also performed well with many betting on their continued success. The online auction market was worth $6.5 billion by the end of 2000, up from $650 million two years earlier, market research company eMarketer reports. It says revenue from online auctions will reach $16.3 billion by 2004. The market was expected to peak as a percentage of total b2c sales in 2000 at 17.6 per cent, declining to 13 per cent in 2004. In December 2000 there were over 1000 retail auction sites in operation, led by eBay.

But exactly what kind of consumer products people want to buy online is open to question. For example there has been an explosion in the number of gardening sites in the UK, but have people warmed to buying plants sight unseen? Or having someone pick their groceries for them? Could the failure of fashion retailer boo.com have been in part because people want to try on clothes before they buy?

NEW ECONOMY SNAPSHOT

A report by American Express says an overwhelming majority of consumers prefer shopping in the high street to shopping online. In a worldwide survey 70 per cent of people said they would probably use the internet to research goods and services but make the final purchase in a bricks and mortar store, with 84 per cent saying they prefer to see a product and its salesperson personally. Twenty-eight per cent of current and future internet users said they already shop online or expect to within the next year. Interest was highest in Hong Kong and Sweden. Security and customer service were among the biggest deterrents cited. About four out of five respondents rated trust in the brand name as one of the most important factors when buying online.

Many of the first e-commerce sites failed to grasp these basic points, and have since paid the price. Since then there's been a rise in interest in business-to-business models, where the market isn't saturated – yet. **E-marketplaces**, where companies cut out the middleman by buying and selling services and goods online, are currently proliferating, some backed by major companies. Forrester Research estimates business-to-business e-commerce will be worth $1.3 trillion by 2003.

NEW ECONOMY SNAPSHOT

By 2004, the Boston Consulting Group says business-to-business e-commerce will generate productivity gains equivalent to one or two per cent of sales; and six per cent by 2010. But the market will only support one to three major e-marketplaces within any given industry segment.

Among the areas of b2b commerce thought most likely to succeed are **e-procurement** sites where companies can shop for the services they need. Research from American Express suggests e-procurement activity is becoming widespread in the USA with 40 per cent of mid-sized firms using the internet to buy equipment and supplies as of December 2000. Forty-two per cent said the best benefit e-procurement offers is faster ordering time, 36 per cent cited convenience and 15 per cent said lower process.

The UK will join Germany in dominating e-marketplaces, predicts Forrester Research, taking 50 per cent of all trade. The report predicts growth rates of around 200 per cent in 2003 alone. Forrester says the automotive, transportation and electronics industries will lead the way. It identified three types of e-marketplace to emerge by 2002: sites aimed at buyers, at sellers and neutral sites for fragmented markets. It says only one in 20 e-marketplace providers will survive the next five years, leaving only 50 European e-marketplaces in total. Forrester predicts six per cent of all b2b trade in the EU will be transacted in e-marketplaces by 2005.

International Data Corporation says the anticipated growth of e-marketplaces has been greatly exaggerated, dismissing calls for thousands of e-markets by 2004 as 'overzealous'. The report says only several hundred e-marketplaces will survive that long.

eMarketer predicts the e-mail marketing industry will be worth $4.5 billion by 2003. The report suggests spending on e-mail marketing will reach almost $1.1 billion by the end of 2000. Spending on e-mail advertising alone is expected to reach $2 billion by 2003. Revenue from e-mail advertising is expected to rise from five per cent of total web advertising in 1999 to 13 per cent in 2003.

Which platform will rule?

Just which platform will be the best for e-commerce? While no one's predicting the death of the PC yet, many are looking to mobile devices and interactive television as the wave of the future. However analysts say it's unlikely that there will be only one winner. Instead, they expect platforms to be complementary, enabling consumers to choose how they want to receive information and when.

The web and web-enabled devices will generate $269 billion in sales, and influence another $378 billion in off-line sales by 2005, according to Forrester Research. The company says PCs should continue to lead with $246 billion in sales in 2005, with interactive television second, followed by mobile devices. In total, non-PC devices are predicted to generate just $23 billion in sales by 2005, but will influence another $128 billion in off-line sales. By 2003 internet-enabled devices are expected to influence $146 billion in off-line sales. In the USA, PC-based sales will total $45 billion in 2000, reaching $154 billion by 2003.

Jupiter research predicts the PC will still be the dominant channel for accessing the internet, with 87 per cent of commercial and advertising revenues, followed by digital TV at 11 per cent and mobile at a mere two per cent. Jupiter predicts the boundaries that have separated internet start-ups and traditional businesses will disappear as the web evolves to a mass-market 'everyday internet'. Jupiter says European businesses have yet to understand how to use the mediums. 'Just as the traditional companies were slow to get on the web, today's web portal e-commerce and content companies have made the mistake of simply distributing their website to interactive TV and wireless without understanding what consumers want from these new mediums,' said Noah Yasskin, Director of European Research. Jupiter predicts that the internet will become dominated by those traditional companies that can successfully make the transition to 'everyday internet' by selling their products and distributing their content on whichever platform their customers choose to use. While many dot-com businesses have failed because they relied solely on revenues generated from the internet, in the future they will either acquire off-line businesses or will be acquired themselves by traditional bricks and mortar companies. The very few pure internet companies left will be niche businesses, it says.

NEW ECONOMY SNAPSHOT

By 2005, there will be 41 million UK mobile internet users, but they are not expected to make substantial online purchases, according to Forrester Research. Of those users 28 million will also use PCs and interactive TVs and will continue to make most of their purchases via the PC. The 12 million others will make simple transactions on their mobiles.

part five
moving forward

chapter fourteen
the world according to you

- ◆ Priorities

- ◆ Desires

- ◆ Telecommuting

- ◆ Freelance/contract work

As we've seen, new economic models stress **strategic alliances** and **networking** over corporations as a monolithic whole. With the decline of the traditional company, so comes the obsolescence of the company man/woman. The New Economy demands that you take control of your own work destiny in a way you might have previously expected from a supervisor or manager. It's nice to have corporate loyalty, but these days it's the corporation of you that should take precedence. As one recruitment agency dubbed it, **Me Plc**.

In order to prosper in the New Economy, you have to **be your own career counsellor**, setting yourself professional development goals to achieve and timetables to get there. Introducing the **portfolio career**, one where you take jobs to acquire specific skills before hopping off to another project. It's a less predictable, less stable work world – but one that offers tremendous opportunities for those who plot their courses carefully. There are certainly risks – but the rewards lead to greater individual career satisfaction than has ever been possible.

Priorities

Ask yourself:

- ◆ What gives me the most satisfaction at work?
- ◆ What type of projects do I like to work on?
- ◆ Do I prefer interacting with people or not?
- ◆ Do I want flexibility or stability?
- ◆ Do I aspire to greater responsibility?
- ◆ Do I aspire to have greater choice in my work?
- ◆ Are the people I work with important to me?
- ◆ How do I learn best? Am I a show-me person or a reader?
- ◆ How do I ensure I stick to a timetable?
- ◆ How do I motivate myself? Do I prefer short-term or long-term satisfaction?

The answers to these questions should give you a fair idea where you stand in general. The first step to moving forward is to embrace the **mindset**. Shake off your allegiances to your team or your company. It may sound harsh, or selfish, but that fact is that the New Economy is here – you can't afford *not* to look out for yourself. Companies these days just can't afford to. However, they are happy to harness your desire to pursue certain mutually acceptable goals. See it as a new partnership between you and your employer, one that's more equal, and that respects your desires.

Now come up with some desires! What part of the work world do you find most appealing? Would you rather work flexible hours or regular shifts? Do you prefer the sociability of the office or the tranquillity of home? Do you favour a high-flying lifestyle or are the trappings of success less important than the consistency of the work? Play to your strengths. In what environments are you most productive?

Desires

Ask yourself:

◆ Where do you want to be next year? In five years? Ultimately?

◆ What would you like your obituary to say?

Once you are clear about your priorities and desires, you can apply them to every decision you make regarding the job you choose. As a good career counsellor would say, set yourself a five-year plan, with intermediate goals along the way. If you need help, ask for impartial advice from family and friends. Be prepared to radically revise the plan along the way, to adopt an attitude of 'creative destruction' if necessary.

Telecommuting and freelance work are two of the options you might choose to explore.

Telecommuting

In high-tech, telecommuting – working from home – is accepted practice in some jobs. With the skills shortage many employers now know they need to be more flexible to attract top talent. BT and Virgin are among the most high-profile companies to allow this in a limited form. If you choose to work from home, you should read up on conventional wisdom about establishing a proper home office and what the tax advantages are. There's also good advice to be had about how to juggle home/work tasks such as the importance of setting up an office that is distraction-free and out of bounds to other family members during working hours. Among the issues to address are:

◆ how to maintain your company profile and continue networking outside of the office-based environment

◆ how to maintain contact with people with whom you can share ideas and the latest tips

◆ how to ensure your status is not diminished and that out-of-sight does not become out-of-mind.

Some telecommuting employees make sure to spend at least one day every week or two in the office to address these concerns.

A study by the Henley Centre found that 30 per cent of the workforce do some work from home, 46 per cent of business people have an office or work area in their home, a third expect to do more work from home over the next few years, nine per cent work from home all the time, one per cent work under a formal telecommuting regime.

Freelance/contract work

Contract and freelance work are common in high-tech areas such as web design. If you can handle the instability that freelance work entails, it can bring you unprecedented freedom and a good salary to boot. Here are the main points to note:

◆ Freelancers get higher day rates than salaried workers, and as a result there's a possibility of working fewer hours overall for the same amount of money.

◆ You are free to pick and choose your projects, bosses and companies. Choose them according to the skills you can acquire as well as the actual work you will be doing. Look ahead to see how this job will move you closer to the next one you want. Be prepared to consider work that is mediocre if the doors it will open are better. Your time on the job is limited anyway.

◆ You must be self-reliant – able to network and drum up new business. You must sell yourself constantly, and maintain your own business infrastructure.

◆ The flip side of freelance life is that you are entirely responsible for your own motivation. If you choose a portfolio career there is no manager to pat you on the back – you must do it yourself. Make sure to reward yourself for a job well done. Share your successes with friends and family who appreciate how hard you have worked. Set achievable goals that will give you momentum

moving forward

from here to e

momentum

to reach for the big ones. Remember that long-term gain can involve short-term pain. It's easier to avoid feeling discouraged if you have set yourself a plan with a goal/reward at the end of it (better job, more money, better lifestyle) and can keep in perspective how close you are to achieving that goal.

◆ Anyone starting a small business must have a head for basic accounting or the sense to hire someone else who's in the know. As your own boss you qualify for lots of tax breaks, so make sure you take advantage of them.

chapter fifteen
making the move

- ◆ Networking
- ◆ Job ads
- ◆ Job sites
- ◆ Agencies
- ◆ Volunteer work

By now you've read up on the latest industry news, picked the job you want to aim for, researched the companies out there and repackaged your résumé and yourself. What's next?

Networking

If there's one thing that defines the New Economy it's networking, and getting your job is no different. You need to be able to communicate and interact with other people to get the inside track on companies and job opportunities. Who you know is just as important in the New Economy as it is in the Old Economy. Be aggressive in developing your **contacts** and using the ones you already have. Here are some tips:

- Networking nights for various industries take place monthly in London – check the trade press for events, conferences and lectures you can attend.

- In order to gather the most information from people, you need to ask smart questions and be an attentive listener. Always take an interest in the people you meet socially. Even a simple dinner party can yield leads.

- Act like a sponge – absorb all the information you possibly can.

- Take notes if necessary. Keep a contact book with each person's details (Personal Digital Assistants are great for this).

- Always have business cards to exchange, and follow up, even with a simple thank-you note.

- Ask contacts for referrals to other people they know.

- Asking about job openings outright may put people off – it's often better to ask for information or advice, and let offers be presented.

- Be aware the people from whom you are asking information are doing you a favour – make the exchange pleasant, and don't waste people's time.

- Be focused, specific and pointed in your questioning. Even the busiest people will usually spare a few minutes for someone bright asking intelligent questions.

- Don't overuse a single source, don't forget to return favours, and make time if others ask you for help.

Check the listings in the trade press for upcoming **conferences**, **trade shows** and **job fairs**. Some agencies have events listed on their websites as well. Have CVs and business cards handy when you go. Refine your self-promotional pitch for recruiters – keep it short and simple. Ask for informational interviews if necessary. Research the companies that will attend.

Job ads

It is certainly worth checking the job advertisements in newspapers such as the *Guardian*'s New Media section and trade press such as

New Media Age and *Revolution*. Never underestimate the importance of tailoring your résumé to suit the job, emphasizing the relevant skills at the expense of unnecessary ones.

Job sites

Online, you can put an e-CV in a variety of places. The number of career sites in the UK has mushroomed in the past few years. Among the most popular, according to internet survey firm Media Metrix, were:

◆ Monster (*www.monster.co.uk*)

◆ Fish4Jobs (*www.jobs.fish4.co.uk*)

◆ Reed (*www.reed.co.uk*)

◆ GoJobsite (*www.gojobsite.co.uk*)

◆ The *Guardian*'s JobsUnlimited (*www.jobsunlimited.co.uk*).

A note about **format** – many people prefer to get résumés within the body of the text, not as an attachment, so it's good to have your CV as a Word document and plain text file that you can cut and paste into the body of an e-mail. Use only true-type fonts at the 10-pt size that will display consistently across all environments, such as Helvetica or Arial. Don't use columns, lines or any other fancy formatting that will be lost in a basic text setting. Be aware many databases will check your résumé by keyword, so include nouns and noun phrases over verbs. E-mail a copy to yourself to check how it displays on your screen. Make sure it's scannable into a database by using clear black print on a plain white background.

For core-IT jobs try:

◆ Jobserve (*www.jobserve.co.uk*)
◆ Jobstats (*jobstats.co.uk*)
◆ *uk.jobs* (newsgroup)
◆ *uk.consultants* (newsgroup)
◆ *uk.jobs.contract* (newsgroup)
◆ *uk.jobs.offered* (newsgroup).

Almost 80 per cent of the world's top 500 companies now recruit new staff on their **corporate websites**, up from 29 per cent in 1998 and 60 per cent in 1999 according to a survey by iLogos Research and recruitsoft.com. About 73 per cent of large European companies recruit on their own sites, so check the websites of the companies you want to work for. While you're there, don't forget to research the company's history thoroughly.

Agencies

There are lots of agencies out there who will represent you, for a price, if not to you, then to your potential employer. Some companies do not want to pay their fees, so take that into consideration. Others, however, regularly use agencies, so make sure to do your homework on what they will offer you in terms of individual attention before letting them represent you. There has been an explosion in the number of agencies specializing in New Economy jobs, not surprising given the skills shortage. You can choose between traditional recruitment companies with a New Media wing or one that concentrates on just New Media jobs. There are even those who specialize in areas such as editorial or marketing. You can find their contact details and URLs in the adverts they frequently take out in the industry press. See Chapter 17 for the agencies' own views on moving into the New Economy.

NEW ECONOMY SNAPSHOT

By 2005, $4 billion annually will be spent advertising jobs online, according to an April 2000 report by Forrester. In the next four years corporate recruiters say they will increase internet spending by 52 per cent, while cutting spending on traditional media advertising and recruitment agencies by 31 per cent. Revenues from online assessment and training will top $2 billion. The report says human resource applications will generate $1 billion of revenue.

Volunteer work

In the absence of a paying job presenting itself to you, you might consider volunteering your services, for example, helping a community group set up a website in your spare time. Not only will you make contacts, you will be able to pad your portfolio with experience.

chapter sixteen
show me the money, etc.

- Salary scales: General New Economy jobs

- Salary scales: Core-IT and web development jobs

- Stock options

- Training

- Other perks

'Most desirable recruits will be able to find well-paid jobs, so potential employers will need to differentiate themselves from the competition. This involves matching recruits' aspirations in far more areas than simply reward – including flexible working and benefits, personal development, culture and working environment.'

PricewaterhouseCoopers' 2000 European Benchmarking Study for technology companies

Let's bust one New Economy myth right away: the instant dot com millionaire is not only a cliché, he or she doesn't exist any more – not unless they cashed in their share options before the April 2000 stock market crash. The New Economy gold rush is over. Furthermore, as more trained staff enter the market, some previously unrealistically high salaries will come down.

That said, surveys show that across the board, jobs in the New Economy pay better, and in some specific areas they pay much better, than their traditional industry counterparts. (In addition to the rates given below, some further details can be found in Chapters 8 and 9, accurate to December 2000. A quick scan of current adverts should reveal the going rates right now.)

'Salaries continue to represent the biggest cost for virtually every company participating in the survey. More than two-thirds of respondents award pay increases substantially above inflation – most noticeably in the Software Development sector.'

PricewaterhouseCoopers' 2000 European Benchmarking Study for technology companies

And there's more. Remuneration in the New Economy doesn't stop with salary – perks are a big part of any financial package as well. It's standard for employers to offer training, scholarship programmes, fitness club memberships and more to attract good staff. Add that up and the overall rewards can be rich indeed.

Salary scales: General New Economy jobs

A comprehensive survey published in May 2000 by Hay Management Consultants found that **heads of e-businesses** are paid a full **40 per cent more** than their peers in traditional organizations. The average cash remuneration for the head of an e-business organization was £140,700 (£149,200 in London), of which £24,300 was a bonus. The average salary and benefits package of their peers in traditional organizations was £100,700, or £111,800 in London.

The trend followed the same pattern further down the chain. **Managers** who head up distinct business functions within e-business organizations (marketers, logistics experts, project managers and customer service specialists) were paid up to **17 per cent more** than their peers across the industrial and services sector. For example, the head of marketing in the traditional sector received average basic pay of £52,600 but his e-peer received £61,700. A traditional head of strategy was paid on average £61,800, but his or her e-commerce equivalent got £71,700.

According to a Computer Services and Software Association study on the IT skills shortage in the UK, 79 per cent of the companies surveyed reported that the skills gap was affecting their salary policy and driving salaries upward.

The study also found that New Economy employees got **better employment benefits overall**. In fact they were 15 per cent more likely to receive benefits than their traditional counterparts. They were six per cent more likely to get general-purpose loans from their employers, 50 per cent more likely to get car loans, 33 per cent more likely to get mortgage subsidies and 20 per cent more likely to get flexible benefits.

Said Hay's managing consultant Iain Smith, 'Entrepreneurial and technical skills are widely perceived as being the keys to commanding a high salary in the e-business world. Traditional business skills, however, such as marketing, once overlaid with new knowledge about how these disciplines are pursued in an internet environment, command significant additional pay.

'Many large established firms setting up e-business operations have sophisticated reward strategies designed to meet not just the financial, but also the practical and emotional needs of the individual,' said Smith.

Salary scales: Core-IT and web development jobs

The core-IT jobs are where the skills shortage has hit hardest. Richard Bowery, Managing Director with recruitment agency Careerplus said, 'Employers keep on to their staff by offering inflated salaries, large bonuses and stock options. A typical web developer's salary has increased by 15 per cent from this time last year to an average of £25,750 … There is a particular shortage of Java developers at present, which has led to companies recruiting C++ programmers with no Java experience to fill these roles. A strong C++ programmer will be able to learn Java within two weeks as the language is very similar.'

Bowery cites the following average salary scales for 2000:

- Web developer £25,750
- Analyst programmer £30,185
- Database developer £29,657
- Testing £27,463
- Business analyst £34,839
- Network administrator £24,850
- PC support £22,157
- Web designer £23,879

Corps Business, a New Media and print recruitment agency, publishes a salary survey covering artworkers, graphic and multimedia designers, web designers and web developers (*www.corps.co.uk*). It identified **web developers** as the hottest property in its 2000 survey – with junior candidates (graduates without any industry experience) being offered salaries of £19,000. 'After the candidate has gained one year's experience they are like gold dust,' the study said. The national average salary being offered was £27,500. Junior **web designers'** salaries were marginally less, starting at £18,300 jumping to £24,000 after two years. The national average salary is £25,100. The survey identified **artworking** (producing standard artwork for advertisements using desktop software) as an easy point of entry for graphic designers, with salaries for entry-level positions around £17,400. Other national average salaries on offer:

- Graphic designers: £22,900
- Multimedia designers: £26,100
- Video and 3D animation: £26,800

Stock options

'One of the major developments over the last year has been the increase of employee share schemes such as stock options. The survey shows that a high proportion of staff now participate in some form of company share scheme.'

PricewaterhouseCoopers' 2000 European Benchmarking Study for technology companies

The volatility in the stock market has made employees a bit less enthusiastic about stock options, which used to be the favourite way for cash-poor dot coms to attract employees and lock them in with a promise of riches following a public offering. These plans typically allowed employees to buy a certain number of shares at a set price following specific periods of service. Employees who bought shares prior to the company going public with an Initial Public Offering (or IPO, which means putting those shares on the open market) reaped huge windfalls during the period when high-tech shares were wildly popular. Since that time the market has cooled and some of those shares have dropped sharply in value. In the wake of the 2000 shakedown many companies cancelled or delayed planned IPOs, and employees are now asking for higher guaranteed salaries. A PricewaterhouseCoopers survey done in August 2000 said, 'Online companies are rewarding top executives with greater total cash (base and bonus) compensation packages than they did last year, while at the same time more carefully granting equity to employees across the board.' It also noted that options were being granted more than once annually, allowing companies to average the strike prices over the year.

Says Richard Bowery of Careerplus, 'There are a variety of share option schemes and different companies may offer different schemes. These vary depending on issues such as cash requirements and tax efficiency. The most recent scheme to receive the backing of Parliament was the Enterprise Management Incentive Scheme, which is a tax-efficient scheme for giving the top 15 key employees/executives share incentives.'

Training

With the skills shortage, many companies find it more cost effective to teach staff new skills than to hire expensive experienced workers. The UK IT industry recruited more graduates in 1999 than ever before, the total rising by 50 per cent to 5000 people, with more people going into e-commerce posts than into traditional IT posts, a trend analysts expect to continue.

Companies such as e-commerce consultancy Razorfish offer individual training plans supervised by mentors, including specific technical skills and softer skills such as leadership. The company recently announced funding for employees' education such as MBAs and in-house scholarships consisting of time and resources for workers with good business ideas relevant to Razorfish.

NEW ECONOMY SNAPSHOT

Analysts at research company IDC say companies that spend time training individuals who do not have the exact technical skills needed can gain a competitive advantage. 'Companies that are best known for attending to their employees' welfare are also the companies with the most consistent business results,' said Dr Michael Boyd, Boston-based manager for IDC's Resourcing Strategies research programme.

'On average organizations provide five days of training per employee per year. More profitable organizations provide more training (six days per employee per year). Not surprisingly, the least profitable organizations provide the least amount of training of all (four days per employee per year).'

PricewaterhouseCoopers' 2000 European Benchmarking Study for technology companies

Bigger companies offer more comprehensive training programmes. With a recent report by IDC predicting a shortfall of some 600,000 networking professionals by 2002, the internet networking company

Cisco recently opened an academy in Brussels to train hundreds of graduates a year in technical and teamwork skills.

Other perks

While it probably won't make or break your decision whether to work for a company, it's interesting to note to what extent some employers have gone to keep skilled staff:

◆ A Montreal-based dot com offers private movie screenings and laundry service.

◆ An Atlanta software developer gave its full-time employees new BMWs.

◆ A New Jersey company offers employees a discount pet-care programme.

While UK software developer AIT offers traditional perks such as training and development, it also offers such off-beat bonuses as weekends away where staff can learn skills such as African drumming. Director of International Capital Dina Gray says, 'What we try to do is make sure AIT is an interesting place to work.' Other typical gestures by UK companies include:

◆ Free snacks, coffee bars, casual office attire policies and casual atmosphere

◆ Social events during or after working hours

◆ Health club/fitness programme memberships

◆ Telecommuting options (explained more fully in Chapter 14)

◆ Flexible working hours.

And don't overlook …

One thing to bear in mind as you negotiate your package: while perks such as the above can be more glamorous, don't forget to look for the basics – some companies provide more mundane items such as health care, pension plans and bonus schemes.

part six
in their own words

new economy players speak

chapter seventeen
what leading recruiters have to say

- ◆ Overall recruitment trends

- ◆ Choosing jobs

- ◆ Recruiters' requirements

- ◆ Skills

- ◆ Selling yourself

- ◆ Making the transition

- ◆ The state of the New Economy

During the course of writing this book I had the opportunity to speak to a variety of UK recruitment agencies, big and small, with a range of specialities. I asked some of the most thoughtful recruiters to share some of their thoughts on a range of topics. Here they are in their own words.

Overall recruitment trends

1. **Let's start with overall recruitment trends. What are the hot jobs right now, what makes them hot and what jobs are likely to be hot in the future?**

Andrew Swift, pricejamieson (*www.pricejam.com*): 'I think it's the sector rather than the specific job. [The] hot sectors currently are wireless, especially infrastructure and ASP … not the content companies who rely on either consumer advertising or e-commerce.'

Natalie Jones, New Media Director, The Media Partnership (*www.the-media-partnership.com*): 'Currently there are about five or six ways to generate revenue on the internet. The hottest jobs … are the ones that allow for selling across all the different models and don't focus teams in one direction only. For example, an account manager who can sell e-commerce solutions, sponsorship and advertising as well as dabbling in content deals will gain a much broader understanding of the internet environment than someone just tasked with selling keywords for a search engine. Additionally, it is likely to be much more satisfying as they can use a broader set of skills and develop true creative, bespoke commercial packages for different clients. With regards to the hottest jobs in the future, my money is on interactive TV. It's not quite up and running yet but the targeting systems you should be able to use will be amazing! It should be possible to target as small a sample as one consumer or the masses depending on your campaign aims. The opportunities for promotional activity are practically limitless; however, no one seems exactly sure of how it will work … but the products are all still in development so give them time.'

Bronwyn McQueen, Senior Consultant, Stopgap, (*www.stopgap.co.uk*): '[The] hot jobs right now are for: 1) anyone with online marketing experience i.e. [anyone who] can put together an integrated online and off-line marketing plan, who can put together online briefs for agencies and is able to manage New Media agencies, etc.; 2) Customer Relationship Marketing specialists (not techies but marketing specialists with CRM or eCRM); 3) product development managers. Hot jobs of the future are for: candidates who have gone through [the] launch phases and can apply best practice.'

Richard Bowery, Managing Director, Careerplus, (*www.careerplus.com*): 'The hot jobs are: 1) marketing – online, branding, 2) programming, 3) business development. The hottest skills within the New Media, e-commerce, m-commerce industry at present are developers with Java, ASP and Perl programming skills. If you posses around two years plus solid experience in these languages you will walk into any dot com or web design agency you wish, not talking into account cultural differences. These skills will still be around in the future and I would recommend anyone looking to get into the New Media arena, who has a technical mind, to pursue a course in these languages, and to take any junior position within a company that offers career progression, even if it means no real IT exposure. Working in an admin job will offer the candidate an inside view into how a New Media company goes about its business. A dedicated person will certainly have the opportunity to move into a position of more interest. Probably the arena for the future is interactive digital TV and with the introduction of broadband it is certainly an industry of the future. The skills cross over from the New Media but developers are working on the DTV platform instead of being web-based. A work placement within companies such as NTL, Telewest or Videonetworks would be a start.'

Susan Howstan, Associate Director, Direct Recruitment (*www.Direct-Recruitment.co.uk*): 'The hot jobs right now are first, senior-level account handlers, creatives, project managers and digital planners on the agency side, as most of our clients who are looking to offer digital solutions as part of their overall offering to new and existing clients really do not have enough New Media expertise in house. Some larger direct and integrated agencies have acquired a ready-made solution but the smaller agencies don't have the budget to do so, so are trying to train existing personnel or recruit expertise in house. This is of course to address the increasing demand from clients to incorporate internet, WAP and interactive TV into their CRM strategy. Second, ECRM consultants – same as above, but generally with companies whose area of CRM expertise lies in data and the systems that drive this activity. Third, marketing managers/customer relationship managers with dot coms as these new, digitally literate companies need to recruit candidates whose skills are founded in the traditional off-line below/through-the-line marketing arena. As for the hot jobs of the future ... I believe that online will not be treated as a totally separate discipline but rather just another route to market and candidates who are currently not New Media literate should make more of an effort to get involved and acquire the skills or be left behind.'

Wayne Searle, Consultant, Michael Page Marketing

(*www.michaelpage.com*): 'The most desirable jobs for anyone wanting to enter the dot com arena are with an established company that is branching out and establishing a dot com business, with the prime role for a marketer being the launch of such a business. There are also two distinct areas that are currently in demand. First, the launch, which can include working with large budgets in a high-profile launch, often including TV advertising and other heavyweight above-the-line advertising. The second "hot" area is working on new channels of communications, for example m-commerce, i.e. WAP communication. This really is at the cutting edge of dot com marketing and is suitable for the more technically minded marketer, while the more creative marketer would be suited to working on the launch of a new product offering or service.'

Choosing jobs

2. **What factors should people consider when deciding whether to apply for these jobs?**

Andrew Swift, pricejamieson: 'Consider the business model of the company, the track record of the senior execs and funding (how much, who from and how much more needed). If the role is with a traditional company [bricks and mortar], then is the e-commerce an experiment? Is it integrated into the company as a whole and how high up does the support/commitment go?'

Bronwyn McQueen, Stopgap: 'It's important to understand the New Media "jargon" and be able to sell yourself accordingly. A lot of the jargon actually refers to traditional marketing techniques and you can overcome potential "barriers" by understanding things such as logfiles, spiders, permission marketing and spamming.'

Richard Bowery, Careerplus: '[People should consider] 1) Their technical ability and mind set. Are they happy being a programmer in front of a computer all day? 2) Are they quick learners? 3) Are they happy to take a low salary just to get into the industry? Can they afford to? 4) The culture and laid-back atmosphere. Unfortunately many New Media companies are young companies in terms of age – if the candidate is looking to change career this may be a problem.'

Susan Howstan, Direct Recruitment: 'Candidates should think about where their skills and strengths lie before applying willy-nilly for online marketing jobs. They should keep abreast of who's doing what and the developments in technology, surf the net themselves and be sure that they don't take the first job that comes along. This year has seen the demise of many a dot com venture so I'd say that security and the opportunity for personal and professional development should be key considerations and not money alone.'

Wayne Searle, Michael Page Marketing: 'Since the collapse of certain dot com businesses, security should be high on the list if you are looking to work for a start-up business – you should certainly be investigating the funding of the business. If the company you are considering is part of an already established larger organization, investigate how committed the senior management are to the dot com venture. This can be difficult to establish but is something you can probe during an interview, or by reviewing recent media coverage. If it is a new dot com start-up, look into the reputation of the senior management. Again this can be difficult to find, but media coverage may give an indication. Finally, as an experienced marketer, evaluate the marketplace – do you feel this company has a viable business proposition taking into account the current marketplace and competition?'

Recruiters' requirements

3. **When you recruit people, what are the range of things you look for? What are your top three requirements?**

Andrew Swift, pricejamieson: '[The question is] difficult to answer directly as we always interview to the client's brief. However the three core areas we look for are: a) personality/culture fit with the employer, b) skill set and c) more difficult to define, but how much more the candidate can add to the company than just the existing job to be done.'

Natalie Jones, The Media Partnership: 'The top three requirements are intelligence, market knowledge, sales/commercial skills. New Media is only taking about the top ten per cent of people from other backgrounds. It is very competitive. If [a candidate is] coming from outside the industry I want them to illustrate that they've done their homework, they've got a favourite site which they can talk knowledgeably about, that they've got an opinion about where WAP is going, etc. They don't have to be right, they just have to have an opinion they can back up with examples and be able to show that they've been tracking the industry press. What I most definitely don't look for is someone who thinks it sounds exciting and expects me to tell them all about it.'

Bronwyn McQueen, Stopgap: 'We specialize in freelance marketing, so it's important to have candidates who have sound reasons for wanting to freelance, who are able to hit the ground running and who are adaptable to various industries. In terms of e-marketing skills candidates need to be able to apply them to the above requirements.

Richard Bowery, Careerplus: '1) Suitability to job in terms of skills, 2) education, 3) personality – will they fit into the culture of the company?'

Susan Howstan, Direct Recruitment: The top three criteria are 'probably no different than they have always been: 1) attitude/approach, 2) personality and skills, 3) experience.'

Wayne Searle, Michael Page Marketing: 'Previous experience is important; however, experience in dot com is going to be limited as it is a relatively new area of business. You should therefore look at the skills you already have that need to be applied in a new start-up, for example, project management – have you been involved in a project and how successful was the delivery of that project? Project management also calls for other important "softer" skills, for example, communication – ability to communicate effectively to senior management – and possibly management skills such as budget control. Market knowledge can also be an important factor – if you have experience in a particular field, such as financial services and are looking to join a financial services dot com, you will certainly be a more attractive options than someone from a fast-moving consumer goods background.'

Skills

4. **What advice would you give to someone who's currently got a job in a traditional industry, perhaps in sales or marketing, who wants to move to a dot com? What skills do they need? How should they get them?**

Andrew Swift, pricejamieson: 'Assuming that the person already has the market or product knowledge then the key difference in successfully working for a dot com is flexibility. Most dot coms have extensive business plans and models but very few survive without change, sometimes dramatic change. Therefore flexibility is essential. The New Media market also changes and adapts far faster than any other we've ever worked with, partially because the technology is changing so quickly and partially because the market is evolving so fast. For example, in the last 12 months, the flavour of the month for funding by venture capitalists has gone from b2c to b2b to exchanges to wireless and is now centred on ASP and infrastructure developers for mobile and wireless.'

Natalie Jones, The Media Partnership: 'Sales and marketing skills are totally transferable, so what they need to do is gen up on the industry, what's hot, who's not, etc. There are a number of good websites about for information and then there's the industry press, which at first they'll have to wade through but will gradually become clearer as they learn more.'

Bronwyn McQueen, Stopgap: 'This is the million dollar question. Things to do would be to read the correct industry media, keep abreast of marketing developments via organizations such as the Chartered Institute of Marketing, etc., explore the net from a marketing communications perspective, attend seminars (and network!) and look for opportunities to develop this skill in their existing job.'

Richard Bowery, Careerplus: 'It is actually relatively easy to cross over if you are sales or marketer in a traditional industry. If you have good sales training it will stand you in good stead. Selling a website is the same as selling anything, you just have to get to know the product (website, trading platform, ISP, etc.). Online marketing is slightly different from traditional print marketing – you will need to have an insight into the technology. Branding and marketing campaigns are obviously the same but you will need to get your head around [the following concepts]: online brand management, traffic management, partnerships, community elements, cross promotion, affiliates. The best way to learn is to read industry news.'

Susan Howstan, Direct Recruitment: 'Nobody is going to hand you a job on a plate so before you make the coveted leap into the dynamic and evolving world of online marketing, do your research, read the trade press, investigate courses, teach yourself new packages, have a go at designing your own website, network, find out what opportunities and types of jobs there are out there, think about the type of environment you prefer to work in, what you are best at, what skills you are currently lacking and write lists! People don't seem to bother writing lists any more, whether it's on paper or on a workstation. I tell candidates to consider their lifestyle as well. Work isn't everything. Of course it goes without saying that a helping hand from a friendly recruitment consultant never goes amiss!'

Wayne Searle, Michael Page Marketing: 'The skills already mentioned [project management, communication, market knowledge] are important, but a general interest in e-commerce is just as important. Start by taking an interest in the current news and technology and getting up to speed on the language that is used so you will sound confident and knowledgeable to a prospective employer. If possible, get involved in e-commerce projects that are happening with your current employer or do this on your own by viewing it as a hobby, maybe setting up your own website for friends and family. But most importantly, keep abreast of the current issues facing e-commerce and form an opinion, for example on why a high-profile site such as boo.com went bust or why lastminute.com have decided to launch an off-line brochure this Christmas.'

Selling yourself

5. **How can people put their best face forward? What skills that they already have should they stress to employers?**

Andrew Swift, pricejamieson: 'Every dot com company is a fast-moving and changing place. For the right person it is exhilarating, for the wrong person it is stressful. Therefore it is key that they show that they have a) the skills needed for the role and b) the personality/aptitude to succeed in the company's environment.

Natalie Jones, The Media Partnership: 'If you are a long way down a career path, changing to New Media could well involve a pay cut. Let's face it, just because you are worth £40,000 a year in a traditional environment where you have eight years' experience and run a huge team, doesn't mean you're worth it to a dot com in an environment where you have never proved yourself. Some of your skills will be transferable, but some won't and you'll be lacking industry experience, so the things that made you valuable in traditional industries don't apply. Hence be aware of the salary implications. The best bet in this case is probably to convince your current company that they should put you to work in their online division (if they have one) or float the idea past senior management of you investigating developing one. This way you get to gain online experience that you can draw on in later interviews in an environment that you know, with people who already respect your skills.'

Bronwyn McQueen, Stopgap: 'You need to find out what the clients' needs are. Make sure you understand the explicit as well as implied needs – and verbalize them to the client. Then demonstrate how your unique features would benefit the client and close!!! 1, 2, 3, 4 of sales ... works every time!

Transferable traditional marketing skills can be things such as direct marketing (CRM, e-mail campaigns), creative, project management skills, and more.'

Richard Bowery, Careerplus: 'Just play to your strengths. Emphasize your wiliness to learn, muck in and do jobs that may seem menial. Be a team player. If you can show any entrepreneurial skills from your past experience then do. Target larger companies that have moved into the internet arena. They will have more time to offer you training. You will then find it easier to move into a dot com down the line. Keep going to interviews – do not give up – you will find your niche.'

Susan Howstan, Direct Recruitment: 'See what I said about skills. I can't stress enough how important preparation, consideration and presentation are to the interview process.'

Wayne Searle, Michael Page Marketing: 'Read the job description *carefully* and draw out the skills and experience you have that match the requirements. These can include project work, communication and other skills such as research, copy-writing – it really does come down to the job description, but certainly if you have worked in the marketplace this is a main area to highlight.'

Making the transition

6. Have you had any clients who have made this transition successfully?

Susan Howstan, Direct Recruitment: 'Yes, I have. The vast majority of candidates I have placed into dot com/New Media agency environments this year have all made it against a background in traditional below-the-line/customer relationships marketing. What has made all of these stand out from the rest, however, is their determination, the fact that they have got off their backsides to find out about New Media, have become active web users, self-financed additional training or indeed taught themselves skills such as

HTML, Flash, Dreamweaver, etc. One of my candidates actually worked for free in the evenings for a small internet company in order to learn and to develop new skills.'

Natalie Jones, The Media Partnership: 'Lots … I started in traditional media myself and I've been in online for a year now. Like I said, lots of skills are transferable – making the jump across doesn't have to be hard – but be realistic about what you can do.'

Bronwyn McQueen, Stopgap: 'We have a number of success stories. They revolve around: clients being flexible and open to training; candidates being flexible and willing to move down a step or two; the classic case of being in the right place at the right time. Some candidates have reached a level where skills become easily transferable, for example having well-developed marketing skills in an industry similar to the one in which the client now wants e-commerce marketing ability.'

Richard Bowery, Careerplus: 'There are a number of stories that could be told. The best one was a press journalist, who is around 55 years of age. His desire was to go write content for websites. Easy you might say? Of course he had great writing, communication and experience, but because he did not have a background on the web and because of his age this proved to be a nightmare. Of course the style of writing for the web is different; he had HTML, storyboarding, knowledge of the internet. He went to around 25 interviews over around six months before he was offered a role, at a junior level. The more interviews he went to the more knowledge he picked up. He now has moved into a senior role and is doing very well.'

Wayne Searle, Michael Page Marketing: '[I've] come across people who have made a successful transition from a traditional company – a major high street bank to the bank's spin-off online service (for example). This is because they had the market expertise.'

Andrew Swift, pricejamieson: 'Yes, many. Some from the media, some editorial, some from consulting, banking, etc.'

The state of the New Economy

7. Any general words of advice about the state of the New Economy?

Andrew Swift, pricejamieson: 'I'm wary of commenting as anything I say would probably be completely out of date [by the time the book is published]. But I suppose that's a comment on the New Economy in itself!'

Natalie Jones, The Media Partnership: 'Have a healthy dose of scepticism when faced with dot com ideas. Not all of them will work. And be realistic about what you can do. A large search engine isn't going to employ you in their business development department if you've never done business development and have no online experience, so look about for roles that do allow you to put your existing skills to work while you develop new ones.'

Bronwyn McQueen, Stopgap: 'In any new industry the market goes up and it goes down. If candidates wish to participate then they cannot be risk averse and [must] take a chance (freelancing is ideal for this!). Even when ventures fold, if candidates have gained experience they will be more marketable than before. Clients are becoming more sophisticated in their "wants" from candidates as the skill base in the arena develops. Salary levels are becoming more market-related as the "supply and demand" principle is starting to even out. Candidates are becoming more sophisticated and more cautious in terms of what opportunities they are willing to become involved in. They are no longer satisfied with low salaries and share options, as often the shares do not materialize as ventures fold.'

Richard Bowery, Careerplus: 'No British dot com has made a profit yet. The market is still very buoyant with a large number of positions vacant. We currently have around 400 vacant positions. There are not enough trained candidates to go around. For example some clients have shelved projects because there are not enough developers to work the projects … Some dot coms have fallen by the wayside due to lack of funding, bad business models or even trying to expand too fast. In general the companies that are making money have a traditional background and have moved into the internet, e-commerce arena.'

Susan Howstan, Direct Recruitment: 'I believe that dot com culture and the networked economy is no fad. We have witnessed quite a few hiccups this year due to the increasing number of internet companies whose goal was the Big Fast Buck and who declared themselves public before they were even profitable (or breaking even in some cases). Forward-thinking companies who continually question their place are more likely, in my opinion, to spot future enterprise situations and be successful.'

Wayne Searle, Michael Page Marketing: 'Enter a new business with care and be prepared for it not to work out. Have a contingency plan and maintain a good skills set to fall back on. Freelancing is becoming increasingly popular for dot com companies, although there is a certain amount of reservation [on the part of companies] due to confidentiality. People who freelance now, in the early stages of the e-commerce world, will be highly desirable in a couple of years time due to their breadth of experience.'

chapter eighteen
what leading companies have to say

Advice from:

- ◆ Mike With, Soccernet
- ◆ Katie Wells, Wideyes
- ◆ Paul Basham, y-creds.co.uk
- ◆ Katharin Strauss, OneSwoop
- ◆ Tony Smith, The Register
- ◆ Sally Webster, bol.com
- ◆ David Ferguson, Zeus Technology
- ◆ Robert Leslie, Iglu.com
- ◆ Owen Tyzack, buyingteam
- ◆ Mel Garfield, ihavemoved.com
- ◆ Michael Smith, Firebox
- ◆ Roy Bliss, Talkcast

- Marcus Marcou, BusinessesForSale.com

- Margaret Amein, Improveline.com

- Barb Upchurch, Loot.com

- Annabel Roaf, The First Resort

- Johanna Walker, confetti.co.uk

- Alexandra Rowley, representing First Tuesday

- Glenn Elliot, YAC.com

- Rob Houghton, reallymoving.com

- Rosie Reed, everywoman.co.uk

- Serena Doshi, Liv4now.com

- Steve Chippington, Shopsmart

- Tim Levene, flutter.com

- Bill Wright, BuildOnline

- Adam Ellis, Moonfruit.com

- Jennifer Burt, babyworld

- Zoe Barnes, GoJobsite

- Norman Smith, Allcures.com

- Sridhar Gowda, Countrybookshop.co.uk

- Adrian Smith, Goodmigrations.co.uk

Here's some advice from the people who know what they're talking about – they already work for UK-based dot coms. The companies they represent are all across the New Economy. I asked them what advice they'd give to someone with no dot com experience, looking to make the leap into the dot com world. Their answers:

Mike With, Editor of leading online football site Soccernet (*www.soccernet.com*): 'First, don't expect to become a millionaire overnight – and if anyone promises that, run like hell. Second, it's quite likely that the skills you already have are transferable online, so work out where and how you could already be working. Third, the one thing that everybody working online has in common is the computer: understand it just enough not to be afraid of it.'

Katie Wells, UK Marketing Manager for Wideyes.co.uk (*www.wideyes.co.uk*), a web-based recruitment company: 'Be ready for anything because anything could be thrown at you. Be prepared to fight for your beliefs – due to the nature of the business, your colleagues will be as strong and opinionated as you are. Be prepared to have fun as your colleagues will also become good friends. [You] don't necessarily need to skill up, you will learn very quickly on the job. Stay focused, remain organized and be prepared for the goal posts to change daily.'

Paul Basham, COO, y-creds.co.uk (*www.y-creds.co.uk*), teenage e-tailing site: 'Surf the net, know the market, buy all your stuff on the net, live, eat and breathe the net. If you are joining a start-up then do your own due diligence – will their business really work? Then the biggest skill is guts – and you either have that or you don't.'

Katharin Strauss, Recruitment Manager for online car-buying portal OneSwoop (*www.oneswoop.com*): 'Be selective and do your best to investigate the financial status of your target companies. If you do not like the idea of risk, try to find dot coms that are backed or wholly owned by larger, more stable businesses. Be open-minded and flexible – if what you're after is structured career progression they will probably not be able to offer it in the early stages of the business. Start broadening your skill base. In your current job, take the initiative to offer your services to projects that will enhance and expand your current skills, or if you can't do so in the workplace think about courses you could take outside of work to do this. Think about where you would add the most value to a young, rapidly growing business and apply for jobs in that area. Get on the web and look for opportunities –

most dot coms will advertise vacancies on the internet, if not on their own site, then on one of the myriad of recruitment-related websites. Contracting can be a good way of exploring the dot com environment without committing yourself for the long term, although if you are already in permanent employment this might not appeal. Talk to recruitment agencies that specialize in your field about inroads to dot com businesses. Use your personal network to find out where the opportunities are – a personal recommendation is usually a great way to get your foot in the door.'

Tony Smith, Managing Editor of online IT news website The Register (*www.theregister.co.uk***):** 'Generally, I'd say read up like crazy on related books. Take a trip to the local Barnes & Noble and come away with a stack of up-to-date books covering your area of interest. The key thing about the net is that technology, business and marketing practices are evolving so quickly, you really need to keep on top of them all – and that means a *lot* of background reading.'

Sally Webster, Human Resources Director at bol.com (*www.uk.bol.com***), major book and music e-tailer:** 'I would suggest they spend as much time learning about the industry as possible, through being online and keeping abreast of latest developments through trade journals, etc. They should also enrol on one of the New Media "induction" courses that are being offered now, for example by the recruitment consultancy called New Media HR. This demonstrates initiative and will give candidates the basic knowledge of industry terminology and processes.'

David Ferguson, Vice President of Products and Technology, software company Zeus Technology (*www.zeus.co.uk***):** 'There's not so much of a "skilling-up" but rather a mental adjustment required. "Can't" is not a word we like to hear or use. You need to have initiative, things are moving so fast that you've got to make your presence felt. You need to inspire confidence in your ability to execute, do that quickly and then maintain it.'

Robert Leslie, Content Manager/Editor with online ski holiday bookers Iglu.com (*www.iglu.com***):** 'Don't play up qualifications and academic achievements, as these are rarely entry criteria for dot coms. A-levels and degrees are all very well but are secondary to real experience, flexibility and passion for the work. Given the climate at the moment within dot coms, sacrifices are being made and salaries may not compete with traditional employers (not to mention the lack of benefits/established bonus schemes, etc.) so it is enthusiasm and a willingness to muck in that count. "Dot com millionaire" syndrome is more fantasy than fact so come into the work with your eyes wide open to the whole picture – the nasty work as well as the cool stuff. The lure of dot coms is understandable but the decision to accept a position or not should be weighed up like any other – working hours, pay reviews, etc. Read the small print, if there is any.'

Owen Tyzack, with buyingteam(*www.buyingteam.com*): 'Many skills that are present in other forms of business can be carried over to internet-based enterprises, for example customer service, marketing, PR and sales are fairly universal skills, no matter what business you are in. If someone wanting to change career has experience in one or more of these skills then with some internet experience/training, employment is likely.'

Mel Garfield, representing ihavemoved.com (*www.ihavemoved.com*), a company that informs people of your new address: 'The best way to get dot com skills and experience is to actually work for one. There are plenty of opportunities out there and my best advice would be to grab one of them with an existing company. I don't believe there is such a thing as a bad experience, because even if the business fails, it will still provide an invaluable experience and insight into what dot coms are like to work for.'

Michael Smith, CEO of Firebox (*www.firebox.com*), specializing in gifts for men: 'Go to networking events like First Tuesday or Boob Night. Read everything you can about the industry – books and magazines (*Industry Standard*, *Red Herring*, *Business 2.0*, *Revolution* and *New Media Age* in particular). Use online sites like netimperative and The Register to stay updated. I am very impressed in an interview if someone has a firm grasp of recent industry developments. One last bit of advice – make the most of the covering letter. This is where you really sell yourself. I rely on this many times more than a CV.'

Roy Bliss, Chief Operating Officer for Talkcast (*www.talkcast.com*), the wireless and telecommunications company: 'It isn't about skilling-up, it's about having the confidence in your own ability. Experience counts for a lot but you need the innate capability to understand what you can and can't deliver to a team to make something work. Passion is great and when supplemented by experience – whether it is dealing with suppliers or customers or serving at McDonald's – then it is a powerful combination.'

Marcus Marcou, Managing Director of BusinessesForSale.com (*www.businessesforsale.com*) which brings together buyers and sellers of businesses: 'Be prepared for contradictions. On the one hand you are throwing everything you have learned out of the window in order to try and understand something that has few fixed models. On the other hand you taking your traditional skill set and experience and applying it accordingly. Talking to your customers is the same experience whether you are a dot com or a bricks and mortar business. Be prepared to roll your sleeves up. Everyone expects glamour. The internet is just not glamorous. It's very technical. It can be very frustrating.'

Margaret Amein, Managing Director of home improvement site Improveline.com (*www.improveline.com*): 'Only take a job with a strong, varied, experienced management team/board.'

Barb Upchurch, Editor of classified advertising site Loot.com (*www.loot.com*): 'If I were interested in moving to a dot com, I would determine where my current skill set would fit, and what I am lacking. This can be done easily by reading the classifieds. I would take classes if needed and read everything about the market, e.g. WAP, digital TV, 3G technology, etc. When these applications take off, there will be a need in the market for skilled employees in these areas.'

Annabel Roaf, Human Resources and Recruitment Manager with online travel agent The First Resort (*www.thefirstresort.com*): 'We want to see proactive people – if they have illustrated this in their current company and their career to date then hopefully they will do the same for us.

Therefore, those people who have actively sought the opportunity to get involved in their company's internet development, even if it doesn't fall within their job requirements, are going to stand out. As well as providing them with valuable experience it shows they have a commitment to developing their skills in this area. Maybe they have proposed ideas and been frustrated because they have been knocked back due to the traditional nature of their current employers. There are numerous courses available but I would not consider these to be a vital element of making the move – unless, of course, you are looking at a highly technical role.'

Johanna Walker, Head of Content and Commerce Operations at major UK wedding portal confetti.co.uk (*www.confetti.co.uk*): 'Get a computer, an HTML manual, a copy of Dreamweaver and an image-editing tool and just build your own site! There are loads of user groups out there swapping hints and tips and offering advice. But do give building something a go before turning up for an interview – there's nothing worse than receiving a CV from someone who has no URLs to show for themselves.'

Alexandra Rowley, Gnash Communications, representing networking group First Tuesday (*www.firsttuesday.com*): 'An eclectic mix of skills is required to succeed in the dot com industry. Experience is needed, but usually, the variety of roles that make up a dot com team attract skills and backgrounds from everywhere. Also, as the New Economy is still in its infancy, it is generally recognized that not every employee will have specialized experience in this new industry. Therefore recruiters are looking for new and innovative skills and backgrounds to mirror the New Economy. Ambition and flexibility are key to the nature of your skills. An ambition and determination to succeed, through any obstacle, is absolutely key to surviving the dot com world … You generally need to be a person unafraid of financial and career risks, depending on the size and age of the company you're joining. The rewards of success in a New Economy are great and additional benefits such as share options are extremely attractive. However, the risks are also many so potential employees must consider their options with their eyes open. If you're keen on making a transition, try and learn as much as you can about the particular industry you're interested in. No one will expect you to be a technical expert but it does pay to show some foresight and knowledge about how your skills can be applied.'

Glenn Elliot, with YAC.com (*www.yac.com*): 'If anyone is thinking of moving to an internet-based industry they must know why they want to make the move. If they have no interest in the net then it is pointless. I believe that the same rules apply to any industry.'

Rob Houghton, Managing Director of moving-home services website reallymoving.com (*www.reallymoving.com*): 'Potential joiners to an e-commerce company should: consider [the] company very carefully and understand its sustainability; be careful about joining on the basis of one individual – people move on very quickly; be prepared to do anything to help the company (admin, etc). Good people are like gold dust, so don't be afraid to play hard to get. For younger people, learn basic computer skills (Microsoft Office, Windows and a web browser) but don't worry about specific programs unless you are looking for a very specific role. Most people who can work with one system learn others pretty fast.'

Rosie Reed, Editor with major women's portal everywoman.co.uk (*www.everywoman.co.uk*): 'Get an understanding of the internet, the concept, the players, where the industry is headed. Read industry press, spend time on the net, think about what sites you like and why. Read the "about us" pages on a variety of websites – they tell you about the site's vision – and then study the site in question and think about whether they are achieving that aim. If not, why not? Be prepared to get in at ground level and be flexible. Most importantly, remember if you have good business skills and experience in a traditional industry they are always valuable. If you have experience in an industry off-line, those skills are applicable to the same industry online. Be confident in that knowledge.'

Serena Doshi, Managing Director of lifestyle portal Liv4now.com (*www.liv4now.com*): 'Be interested for the right reason – it's hard work but an enlightening experience. Make sure you enjoy the specific area that the company is involved in as you may spend a lot of time doing it! Start reading quality publications that cover the internet. I find *Industry Standard* a great magazine for the latest internet news, and the *Wall Street Journal (Europe)* is also a good newspaper. There are also helpful internet e-mail newsletters, which are free to sign up for and will help on the up-to-date on internet occurrences. Yahoo! Finance is indispensable as a source of information as well.'

Steve Chippington, Marketing Director with online price comparison service Shopsmart (*uk.shopsmart.com*): 'Just jump in. It is very different but really refreshing for those people who like a challenge. Anyone who likes procedures and needs to look at last year's plan should avoid the market.'

Tim Levene, Director of Business Development at person-to-person betting site flutter.com (*www.flutter.com*): 'You will need the core skills to do the job asked. For example, you're in a marketing role for a traditional business but want to work for a consumer dot com. Have you researched the b2b and c2c market? Do you know who the players are? Have you researched e-brands or e-marketing techniques? Basically know the market you want to move to as much as possible and be able to demonstrate that in your applications.'

Bill Wright, Business Development Manager for building industry e-commerce site BuildOnline (*www.BuildOnline.com*): 'People looking for a way into a dot com need to understand … that the recruiting stage of a dot com may not be as streamlined as in more established businesses. They need to be aware that dot coms require their employees to be able to adapt to a changing, dynamic, and rapidly growing environment. Once work has commenced they need to be prepared for a very direct communication style and fluid processes. I would recommend that they ensure that they do some research and have an understanding of how technology and the internet can affect their traditional industry of experience and look to how their experience can bring added value. This can be done by reviewing specialist magazines or reports, participating in seminars or training courses aimed at providing general information about the e-commerce world and by inquiring about work placements or internships.'

Adam Ellis, Head of Human Resources, online website-building community Moonfruit.com (*www.Moonfruit.com*): 'The most important advice about changing jobs is to understand and know what you are looking for in your next job. You should then consider whether the companies you are targeting from a recruitment perspective are going to satisfy your requirements. Second, you need to assess whether the business model that the company has adopted is going to work and be successful. The best way of doing this is to ask about their funding status and check up on their recent press articles. Finally, really research the business, ask friends and take up some references on them.'

Jennifer Burt, Editor of child-rearing portal babyworld (*www.babyworld.co.uk*): 'I would look for a company that had a history in the dot com world or had non-dot com backers (Freeserve, who I work for, came from Dixons). It offers a little stability in a very volatile world to know that you have a well-established company behind you. In terms of skill, it depends on the job you are looking for. If it's a technical job and you have no relevant training then complete retraining will be on the cards. If it is, for example, an editorial job, then publishing background and familiarity with normal software packages will be the foundations of your application. Then it's just a case of marking yourself out from the crowd, as with every job application!'

Zoe Barnes, GoJobsite, popular online job-listing website (*www.gojobsite.co.uk*): 'In general [candidates] must be able to demonstrate a good understanding of the potential of the internet. Overall I think that being able to convey enthusiasm for the products, services and experiences that the prospective dot com has to offer is vital. Regarding skills, I don't think that there is any need to "skill yourself up". Clearly if you are planning to apply for a position in the IT department and you've never seen a computer before then there's a very long road ahead for you, as well as very little hope. Otherwise, so long as you have good personal skills, efficient computer skills, you know the internet well and you are a fast learner then there should be no reason why you can't fit in from almost any other industry sector.'

Norman Smith, Allcures.com (*www.allcures.com*), online pharmacy and health information: 'Computer literacy is an essential in all walks of life but a greater understanding of hardware functionality would be advantageous. The speed of action required in the dot com world doesn't give time to wait for a techie to fix it.'

Sridhar Gowda, co-founder, book e-tailer Countrybookshop.co.uk (*www.Countrybookshop.co.uk*): 'Knowledge and experience gained in traditional industries are valuable and can easily and naturally be applied to the dot coms. [Candidates] should research in their industry and find out how their industry and competitors are embracing the New Media and keep up to date with the developments by joining the relevant newsgroups, newsletters, and reading relevant magazines and books.'

Adrian Smith, researcher with Goodmigrations.co.uk (*www.goodmigrations.co.uk*), a portal for people moving home: 'Be prepared to work hard with the potential for high reward. No special skills [are] required (if it's a non-IT position). The general principles of the business are the same as traditional companies, just faster.'

chapter nineteen
what new economy workers have to say

- David Ferguson, Zeus Technology

- Jennifer Burt, babyworld

- Mike With, Soccernet

- Adam Ellis, Moonfruit.com

- Sally Webster, bol.com

- Annabel Roaf, The First Resort

- David Gilroy, Sift

- Johanna Walker, confetti.co.uk

- Marcus Marcou, BusinessesForSale.com

- Michael Smith, Firebox

- Owen Tyzack, buyingteam

- Paul Basham, y-creds.co.uk

- Rob Houghton, reallymoving.com

- Robert Leslie, Iglu.com

- Steve Chippington, Shopsmart

- Tim Levene, flutter.com

- Tony Smith, The Register

- Mel Garfield, ihavemoved.com

- Paul Rogers, Liv4now.com

In this chapter, some of the contributors to the book explain how they themselves made the transition to the New Economy.

David Ferguson, Vice President of Products and Technology, Zeus Technology (*www.zeus.co.uk*): 'I first met one of the founders of Zeus in 1995. The summer that Adam and Damian started the company, Adam spent the summer writing software for me at Madge Networks. We lost contact afterwards but then I stumbled across his name on an article on the internet and decided to find out whether this was the Adam that I knew. We met up for lunch, I lamely pitched the services that my then employer could offer Zeus and then proceeded to inquire into openings that Zeus might have. A funding round and a few months later, I had an interview, I was offered the role and I immediately accepted. Why? I'd set myself some goals in my next role – responsibility in a well-funded internet start-up. Zeus met those entirely. I've had an amazing ten months here – we're in the middle of our second office move, the company has nearly quadrupled in size and we're on our way to being extremely successful.'

Jennifer Burt, Editor, babyworld (*www.babyworld.co.uk*): 'I trained as a journalist at postgraduate level and worked on a small evening paper then a very large evening paper, rising to news desk and health correspondent. I took maternity leave for the birth of my first child but felt unhappy with the hours required on an ever-changing basis as it made childcare difficult if you didn't know from one week to the next what shifts you were working (my partner worked even more random shifts). I applied

from here to e

momentum

for the editorship of babyworld where my journalistic background (particularly health) and my parenting knowledge were the key factors in getting the job, as I was very enthusiastic about the topic but had the skills to back it up. Why did I move to dot com? It was the right job at the right time – and although I might move back in the future, I would sorely miss the ability to react instantly to news and problems instead of three times a day in a print run!'

Mike With, Editor, Soccernet (*www.soccernet.com*): 'I was working for a premium-rate telephone company – essentially the "new media" of the day – and left when I realized they weren't moving quickly enough in response to the fast-arriving internet. Having been a sports journalist, I was able to take those skills and experience and apply them to the internet at a quite early stage in its development.'

Adam Ellis, Head of Human Resources, Moonfruit.com (*www.Moonfruit.com*): 'One of the most demotivational factors of working in a large corporate business is the inability for young bright entrepreneurs to contribute to the direction and success of the business. I left a big corporate company, as it was hard to add value to an established product, to try my hand at something new. Arriving at Moonfruit presented me with a real challenge to show people what I could do, as it was a real greenfield site with no systems, processes or procedures set up. It has been great to start things off from scratch, if not a little exhausting. The challenge has been in facilitating and enabling a rapidly moving business to achieve its objectives with the minimum amount of bureaucracy and the maximum amount of fun.'

Sally Webster, Human Resources Director, bol.com (*www.uk.bol.com*): 'I moved into New Media from the record industry (I previously worked for BMG Entertainment). I first joined AOL and was attracted to the sector as it was clearly demonstrating enormous potential for explosive growth, like no other industry of our time. I was simply attracted by the challenge that this would undoubtedly present from the HR perspective, and the opportunity to be part of something groundbreaking.'

Annabel Roaf, Human Resources and Recruitment Manager, The First Resort (*www.thefirstresort.com*): 'I had been working as a Recruitment Consultant and wanted to move to a company where I could utilize my recruitment skills but where I would have genuine opportunity to progress to human resources. From my point of view this was a fantastic opportunity because I would be joining a new company where I would be responsible for recruiting everyone else (there were four people when I joined!). I was given the freedom to establish my own procedures for recruitment and from day one also took on all the human resources work. If I had joined a large, established company, it would have taken me two years to get where I have in six months. I was introduced via an agency. What made me the successful applicant? I think it was in part the recruitment experience I had but was largely due to the ideas that I put forward and the fact that I relished the challenge that they were proposing. They recognized my potential to progress quickly and my ability to represent the company in the right manner.'

David Gilroy, Operations Director, Sift (*www.sift.co.uk*): 'After graduating with an engineering degree in 1987 I quickly realized engineering was not "where it was at". I then joined Reuters as a management trainee and ended up working in Customer Support. I left there in late 1991 to join CompuServe as Customer Services Manager (where I met Andrew Gray). I left CompuServe UK to move to the US HQ in late 1995. I was only there six months as Andrew and I both decided to leave and set up Sift. That was four years ago and the rest is history.'

Johanna Walker, Head of Content and Commerce Operations, confetti.co.uk (*www.confetti.co.uk*): 'I was working as a communications manager in New York in 1997 and started using the internet for shopping, etc. and also as a means of communication for work purposes – I ended up building a site and project managing the development of another and knew I really wanted to get into the internet full time. While browsing the *Guardian* online job site (of course!) I saw a vacancy advertised for AOL – in the UK! I moved back home and basically begged them to give me a job as the producer of their new Shopping Channel, and the rest, as they say, is history!'

Marcus Marcou, Managing Director, BusinessesForsale.com (*www.businessesforsale.com*): 'How did I get into the dot com world? Pure good fortune. The good idea was already there. I am simply a caretaker of a good idea. Let me explain. My family used to publish a magazine called *Businesses For Sale* – it did okay but was not going to set the world alight. However, the internet site BusinessesForSale.com has become a spectacular success on the simple basis that people looking to buy or sell a business find our site because they type "Businesses For Sale". There is no need for us to spend on advertising or marketing. This is the good fortune. Turning that good fortune into a multi-million pound business is down to hard work and good strategy. Life is just like backgammon – every one of us at some point will roll a double six. If you play backgammon for long enough you will roll a double six. Question: Will you know what to do when your double six comes up? I'd like to think that we are in the process of turning our double six into a winning position.'

Michael Smith, CEO, Firebox (*www.firebox.com*): 'I set up the business with a friend of mine, Tom Boardman, after university. We wanted to set up a business that would be fun to run but that also exploited an untouched niche. We didn't have a great deal of financing and so needed to sell products that got a lot of free publicity. The internet also made sense as a channel since we couldn't afford a shop or mail order catalogue. The company is growing at a phenomenal rate and things are looking great. We're loving every minute!'

Owen Tyzack, buyingteam (*www.buyingteam.com*): 'I graduated with a history degree, so the internet was not the stereotypical choice of career for a graduate in my discipline; however it is fast moving and exciting and will be very influential in years to come. Although sometimes reported as being unstable, the majority of positions are secure, providing skills and experience that are both sought after and highly transferable.'

Paul Basham, COO, y-creds.co.uk (*www.y-creds.co.uk*): 'I am an accountant by training and I was looking for a new challenge. I spent a year in the USA in 1998 and saw the massive power, scope and influence of the net and decided that was *the* space to be in for 1999. An old colleague had his own start-up and a few drinks led to a job – on no salary! Look before you jump but then you really do have to jump!'

Rob Houghton, Managing Director, reallymoving.com

(*www.reallymoving.com*): 'I worked as banker/consultant in the telecoms/internet field and was keen to set up my own company at some point. Moved house early 1999 – a disaster – and launched reallymoving.com as a means of helping others avoid such disasters.'

Robert Leslie, Content Manager, Iglu.com (*www.iglu.com*): 'I wanted to learn about the internet and was a passionate skier anyway. [This was an] opportunity to take a non-specific role and carve out my own position. I work in marketing, business development, editorial and web design. Small dot coms will allow you width and possibilities that you may not find anywhere else.'

Steve Chippington, Marketing Director, Shopsmart

(*uk.shopsmart.com*): 'I wanted a new challenge and need a fast-moving business environment. My background is consultancy, retail, movies and TV so I believe that I have the ideal combination of streetwise and strategic. I like new challenges and blue-sky thinking. I love the need to do it now and shaping the future. Why do you, the reader, want to leave the traditional environment?'

Tim Levene, Business Development Director, flutter.com

(*www.flutter.com*): 'From a personal point of view I joined flutter as the first employee back in October 1999. I knew both the founders, who pitched me the idea that simply blew me away. We are now 90 and growing slowly but surely. I ran a retail business and had no intention of selling it off but the attraction to joining flutter was that I believed that this could be one of the most exciting e-businesses to date. My previous job before setting up my own business in 1997 was at Bain & Co. the management consultants, which took me to Moscow, Sydney, Boston, Hong Kong and London. The team we have built here is one of the best in the industry and that really has been a focal point in recruiting from the start.'

from here to e

momentum

Tony Smith, Managing Editor, The Register (*www.theregister.co.uk*):
'I've been a journalist covering the information technology sector for over ten years. I moved into the dot com arena by accident rather than design – though I'd thought in the past it would be a good sector to get into – simply by being offered my current post out of the blue by the site's editors. It's the old adage: it's not necessarily what you know, but who you know. That may be an Old Economy statement, but it's just as applicable in the new one.'

Mel Garfield, representing ihavemoved.com (*www.ihavemoved.com*):
'I got into the business by doing an MBA at the London Business School. I heard a lot about the internet while I was studying there and decided to take advantage of the relevant courses that were to do with it. It was really this that sparked my interest and made me think about the opportunities out there.'

Serena Doshi, Managing Director, Liv4now.com (*www.liv4now.com*):
'Liv4now.com's Editor Paul Rogers joined the company in 1999 from *GQ* magazine where he was a sub-editor with significant editorial and journalistic skills, but minimal internet experience. Within an extremely short space of time, Paul moved up a steep learning curve, "real-time", and can now operate various software applications, for example, using the company's internal systems to publish articles from members and writers, write html code. He even administers live online events in with the company's auditorium chat software.'

appendix one
where to go for more info

- General New Economy
- Computer/technology press
- Marketing, advertising and PR
- Networking and associations
- Research institutes
- HTML
- Job boards and career counselling sites
- Career development sites
- Recruitment agencies
- Contracting/consultants
- Books
- Fun

General New Economy

Business 2.0 magazine (*www.business2.co.uk*, US version
    www.business2.com)
E-commerce Times website (*www.ecommercetimes.com*)

e-first magazine (*www.e-first.com*)
Edupage mailing list (*www.educause.edu*)
Fast Company magazine (*www.fastcompany.com*)
Industry Standard magazine (*www.thestandardeurope.com*, US version *www.thestandard.com*)
internet business magazine (*www.ibmag.co.uk*)
Internet Investor magazine (*www.internetinvestor.co.uk*)
internet investor newsletter (*www.internetinvestorUK.com*)
netimperative website (*www.netimperative.com*)
New Media Age magazine (*www.nma.co.uk*)
Red Herring magazine (*www.redherring.com*)
The Register.co.uk (*www.theregister.co.uk*)
Revolution magazine (*www.revolution.haynet.co.uk*, US version *www.revolutionmagazine.com*)
UK internet.com website (*www.uk.internet.com*)

Computer/technology press

CNET (*www.cnet.com*)
Computer Weekly magazine (*www.computerweekly.com*)
New TV Strategies magazine (*www.nma.co.uk*)
PC Magazine (*www.zdnet.com/pcmag/*)
Wired magazine (*www.hotwired.com*)
Ziff-Davis (*www.zdnet.com*)

Marketing, advertising and PR

Advertising Age magazine (*www.adage.com*)
Clickz website (*www.clickz.com*)
Emarketer website (*www.emarketer.com*)
Guerrilla Marketing portal (*www.gmarketing.com*)
Marketing magazine (*www.marketing.haynet.com*)
Marketing Age magazine (*www.mad.co.uk*)
Marketing Online portal (*www.marketing-online.co.uk*)
Marketing Week magazine (*mad.co.uk*)
PR Week magazine (*www.prweek.com/uk/*)
uk-netmarketing mailing list (*www.chinwag.com/uk-netmarketing*)
uknm-jobs mailing list (*www.chinwag.com/uknm-jobs*)
uknm-roundup mailing list (*www.chinwag.com/uknm-roundup*)

Networking and associations

Boob Night (*www.boobnight.co.uk*)
Computer Services and Software Association website
  (*www.cssa.co.uk*)
First Tuesday (*www.firstuesday.com*)
UK New Media events mailing list (*www.chinwag.com/uk-events*)
WAPwednesday (*www.wapwednesday.com*)

Research institutes

Datamonitor (*www.datamonitor.com*)
Fletcher (*www.fletcheradvisory.com*)
Forrester (*www.forrester.com*)
IDC (*www.idc.com*)
Jupiter (*www.jup.com*)
MMXI Europe (*www.mmxieurope.com*)
NetValue (*www.netvalue.com*)
Nua Internet Surveys (*www.nua.ie*)

HTML

Cnet's Builder (*www.builder.com*)
Developer.com (*www.developer.com*)
NSCA (*www.nsca.com*)
Unique HTML Guide (*html-guide.home.ml.org/intro.html*)
Web Developer's Virtual Library (*www.stars.com*)
Webmonkey (*www.webmonkey.com*)

Job boards and career counselling sites

Big Blue Dog (*www.bigbluedog.com*)
Fish4Jobs (*www.jobs.fish4.co.uk*)
GoJobsite (*www.gojobsite.co.uk*)
The *Guardian*'s JobsUnlimited (*www.jobsunlimited.co.uk*)
JobMagic (*www.jobmagic.com*)
Jobs.co.uk (*www.jobs.co.uk*)
Jobserve (*www.jobserve.co.uk*)

Jobstats (*jobstats.co.uk*)
JobTrack Online (*www.jobtrack.co.uk*)
Monster (*www.monster.co.uk*)
Planet Recruit (*www.planetrecruit.com*)
Reed (*www.reed.co.uk*)
uk.jobs newsgroup
uk.jobs.offered newsgroup

Career development sites and publications

Alec (*www.alec.co.uk*)
Cornell's Work Index (*www.workindex.com*)
New Monday website (*www.newmonday.co.uk*)
The Riley Guide (*www.dbm.com/jobguide*)
SkillServer training information website (*www.skillserver.com*)
What Color is Your Parachute? (*www.tenspeed.com*)

Recruitment agencies

Agency Central (*www.agencycentral.co.uk*)
Careerplus (*www.careerplus.com*)
MajorPlayers (*www.majorplayers.co.uk*)
The Media Partnership (*www.the-media-partnership.com*)
pricejamieson (*www.pricejam.com*)
Stopgap (*www.stopgap.co.uk*)
Wideyes (*www.wideyes.co.uk*)

Contracting/consultants

Contracter UK (*www.contractoruk.com*)
Freelance H.Q. (*www.freelance.com*)
Gis-a-Job (*www.gisajob.com*)
uk.consultants newsgroup
uk.jobs.contract newsgroup

Books

Tony Gunton, editor (1994) *Penguin Dictionary of Information Technology*, 2nd edn, Penguin Books

Valerie Illingworth (1997) *Oxford Dictionary of Computing*, 4th edn, Oxford University Press

Kevin Kelly (1999) *New Rules for the New Economy: 10 Radical Strategies for a Connected World*, Penguin USA

Angus J. Kennedy (2000) *The Rough Guide to the Internet*, 6th edn, Rough Guides

Rick Levine *et al.* (2000) *The Cluetrain Manifesto*, ft.com

Christopher Meyer and Stan Davis (1999) *Blur: The Speed of Change in the Connected Economy*, Little Brown and Company

Louise Proddow (2000) *Heros.com: The Names and Faces behind the Dot com Era*, Trafalgar Square

Don Tapscott *et al.*, editors (1998) *Blueprint to the Digital Economy: Creating Wealth in the Era of E-Business*, McGraw-Hill Professional Publishing

Fun

Need to know website (*www.ntk.net*)

appendix two
glossary of common new economy terms

Ad impressions – Number of times a banner ad is downloaded/seen by a viewer.

ASP – Application Service Provider. A company which allows you to access various applications for a price, rather than purchasing the programs outright.

Bandwidth – Expressed in bits per second. The size of the pipeline carrying data. The bigger, the better.

Banner ads – The 468x60 pixel rectangular ads that are the standard for web page advertising.

Bluetooth – Short-range radio chip enabling wireless devices to talk to each other.

Bricks and mortar – Term for traditional retailer whose shop has a physical presence on the high street, unlike pure e-tailers, whose shops exist only on the web.

Broadband – High-speed transmission channel, capable of carrying more than one type of signal at once.

CGI – Common Gateway Interface. A standard way for the web server to get an application program and generate a web page, query a database or perform other interactive tasks.

Click-through rates – Describes the number of people who click on a banner advertisement.

Clicks and mortar – Used to describe a company that blends over-the-web e-commerce with traditional high street retailing (bricks and mortar businesses).

Cold Fusion – Commercial database application that allows databases to be queried through a web browser.

Convergence – The coming-together of technologies into one stream.

CPM – The rate at which an advertiser is charged measured as the cost per thousand impressions.

Datamining – Using software to extract patterns of customer behaviour from databases that store vast amounts of information.

Digital economy – The part of the economy that is related to information presented in digital, as opposed to analogue form.

Domain name – The last part of a web address, divided into such categories as the country you come from (.uk) or the kind of organization you represent (.com or .org).

Dot com – Business that exists on the internet, not on the high street.

DSL – Digital subscriber lines. The high-speed copper phone lines capable of carrying much more data than common copper lines. Allow people to receive up to 6.1 Mbps, but more typically about 1.5 Mbps to 512 Kbps downstream and 128 Kbps upstream. ADSL or asynchronous digital subscriber lines allow up to 6Mbps downstream and 640 kbps upstream.

DVD – Digital Video Disks. Disks that can store more information than CD-ROMs. Used to distribute movies.

E-commerce – Electronic commerce, which covers any transactions that would formerly have taken place face to face or by phone, which now take place across the internet.

E-marketing – Marketing on the internet, using banner ads, search engine keyword placements and the like.

Ethernet – The technology used to link computers across a Local Area Network.

FTP – File Transfer Protocol, or the protocol used to upload and download files from one computer to another over the internet.

GIF – Graphic Interchange Format, a common compression format for graphics on the web. Sophisticated GIFs imitate animation.

HTML – HyperText Markup Language, the computer codes used to generate hypertext documents for the web. More sophisticated version is DHTML or dynamic HTML, which has more interactive options.

Interstitial – Also known as a pop-up ad, an interstitial generates itself as a separate web page when the user clicks on a site.

IP – Internet Protocol. The way data moves on the internet. Data is broken into packets that regroup once they reach their final destination.

ISP – Internet service provider. A business selling access to the internet. Increasingly these companies are trying to differentiate themselves by offering additional services such as home pages and local information.

Java – Platform-independent programming language invented by Sun Microsystems which lets you create and use applets (small application programs sent with web pages).

JavaScript – Programming language that lets you add dynamic functionality to pages.

JPEG – Joint Photographic Experts Group. Another common format for graphics on the web. Supports more colours than GIFs.

Linux – Open-source desktop operating system, hoping to challenge Windows. (Operating systems manage the computer's functions.)

M-commerce – Mobile commerce. The ability to conduct commercial transactions over the internet via non-fixed systems, by mobile phone or other wireless devices.

MPEG – Motion Picture Experts Group. Compressed video or audio format.

Multimedia – Computer applications combining several forms of media, such as sound, text and animation.

New Media – As opposed to old media such as print, radio and television, New Media uses digital formats.

Newsgroup – A discussion group made up of messages posted on a bulletin board in a part of the internet called Usenet.

Page views - Number of times a page is requested.

PDA – Personal Digital Assistants. Handheld, wireless organizers such as Psion or the PalmPilot.

Peer-to-peer network – A network such as Napster without a designated central server. Each computer stores files that can be accessed by others in the network.

Portal – Website where users go to be directed elsewhere. Includes search engines and directories.

Protocol – A standard or sets of rules by which two computers communicate.

RAM – Random Access Memory. The area of memory most easily accessed by the computer, used to run most programs. Data here is usually erased when the computer is shut off.

ROM – Read-Only Memory. Where data is stored for good.

Server – Computer that hosts data and is linked by communications lines.

SMS – Short Messaging Service. Allows you to send and receive short text messages on mobile phones or PDAs.

SQL – Standard language that lets you create, manage and query a relational database, where information is organized into tables.

Stickiness – The ability of a site to keep viewers.

T-commerce – Commerce using the interactive television platform.

URL – Uniform Resource Locator. The web's address system, specifying where a certain site can be found.

Viral marketing – Ads that propagate themselves as users pass them on to each other, intentionally or not.

WAP – Wireless Application Protocol. The standard that lets devices communicate through the airwaves.